ADVENTISM
AND
ARMAGEDDON

Have we misinterpreted prophecy?

Donald Ernest Mansell

Pacific Press® Publishing Association
Nampa, Idaho
Oshawa, Ontario, Canada

Edited by Glen Robinson
Designed by Tim Larson
Cover art by Liz Pyle © Image Bank

Copyright © 1999 by
Pacific Press® Publishing Association
Printed in the United States of America
All Rights Reserved

Accuracy of all quotations and references is the responsibility of
the author.

Mansell, Donald Ernest, 1923-
    Adventists and Armageddon : have we misinterpreted
prophecy? / Donald Ernest Mansell.
        p.   cm.
    ISBN 0-8163-1684-8
    1. Seventh-day Adventists—Doctrines 2. Armageddon—
Biblical teaching.   3. Bible—Prophecies—Armageddon.
I. Title.
BX6121.M36 1999
236'.9—ddc21   98-40667
                                                          CIP

99 00 01 02 03 • 5 4 3 2 1

This book is dedicated to
Vesta West Mansell, my beloved wife and best friend.

CONTENTS

ONE

MILLENNIUM MANIA AND FAILED FORECASTS

As the world approaches the year 2000, many Christians believe it will mark the end of six thousand years since Creation and usher in the seventh millennium—the thousand years of Revelation 20. Seventh-day Adventists believe that Christ's coming is near, but we set no dates—or at least we shouldn't. We believe that when Christ comes, He will resurrect the righteous dead, change the righteous living, and take His people to heaven where they will spend the next thousand years. At the Second Advent the living wicked will be destroyed by the brightness of Christ's coming and the desolated earth will become Satan's prison for a thousand years.

Evangelicals have a totally different concept of the millennium. Most believe that the beginning of the thousand years of Revelation 20 will see "God's wrath on the earth," climaxing "at the Battle of Armageddon" and "followed by the millennial reign of Christ" on this earth.[1]

Regardless of differing concepts, as we approach the year 2000, most Christians, including Seventh-day Adventists, feel that this world is on the verge of profound changes. This is not the first time Christians have approached a millennial year expecting great changes to occur. A similar air of expectancy spread throughout Christendom as the year 1000 approached.

More than five hundred years before that memorable year, Augustine, the influential bishop of Hippo, wrote a book, *De Civitas Dei* (On the City of God), in which he set forth a new theory of the millennium. According to this view, the thousand years of Revelation 20 began at Christ's first advent and would end at His second coming a thousand years later, in other words, in the year 1000. Augustine's book exerted a profound influence on Christians of the early Middle Ages. They believed that Christ would return in glory, accompanied by cataclysmic events, and that the Battle of Armageddon would then be fought.

In his book, *Science, Prophecy and Prediction,* Richard Lewinsohn describes the millennial fever that possessed Christendom at the approach of the year 1000:

> The number 1000 oppressed Europe like a nightmare. A wave of fatalism seized the people: the great cataclysm was about to engulf the world. . . . Whole towns repaired to church as one man, or assembled round crucifixes under the open sky, there to await God's judgment on corporately bended knees.[2]

As the world approaches the year 2000, millennium mania and Armageddon anxiety seem to be affecting many Christians.

Unfulfilled Predictions

Ever since Jesus ascended to heaven and promised His disciples He would return, His followers have had a tendency to set dates for His coming. They have done this despite His admonition that, while His followers would know by the signs He gave when His coming was *near*, they would *not* know the "day and hour," or the exact "times and the seasons" (Matt. 24:26; Mark 13:32; Acts 1; 6; 7; 1 Thess. 4:46–5:1).

Because Seventh-day Adventists emphasize the doctrine of the Second Advent, some of us have had an inclination to predict when the Second Coming will occur or when certain eschatological events will happen. This has been characteristic of individuals as well as groups of Adventists ever since the 2,300 prophetic days, or literal years, of Dan. 8:14 ended in 1844. However, this tendency seems to have become more pronounced during the past fifty or sixty years. Here are some examples:

During the late 1930s and early 1940s, while World War II was being fought, some Adventists thought that 1944—the hundredth year since the Great Disappointment of 1844—might be the year of Christ's return. That year, of course, came and went and nothing happened.

In the late 1940s and early 1950s a man in northern California predicted that Christ would come in 1953—or before. Asked how he arrived at this date, he replied that the book, *The Desire of Ages,* pp. 632, 633, says that

> At the close of the great papal persecution, Christ declared, the sun should be darkened, and the moon should not give her light. Next, the stars should fall from heaven.... He [Christ] says of those who see these signs, "This generation shall not pass, till all these things be fulfilled." These signs have appeared. Now we know of a surety that the Lord's coming is at hand....

Christ continues, pointing out the condition of the world at His coming:

"As the days of Noah were, so shall also the coming of the Son of man be. . . ."

Our brother reasoned thus: The last of these celestial signs was the meteoric shower of 1833. The days during which Noah preached that a flood was coming were 120 years, therefore as the days of Noah were 120 years, so it would be 120 years until the Second Coming. In other words, Christ would come in 1953—or before. Before, because Romans 9:29 says that God will cut short His work in righteousness. However, 1953 passed long ago and now no one hears about this prediction anymore. Some forecasts have not had even as much logic as this one.

A few years after 1953, some thought that Noah's 120 years began in 1844 and would end in 1964—just over one hundred years since the General Conference was organized. But that year, too, came and went and nothing happened.

A couple of decades ago, some Adventists believed that 1987 was a jubilee year and that it would mark the beginning of certain eschatological events connected with the national Sunday law. But that year passed and the proponents of this view have had nothing more to say about their predictions.

Beginning in the late 1980s and the early 1990s, some assumed that 1844 must have been a jubilee year, and because 1994 would be the third jubilee since 1844, certain end-time events were sure to occur that year. After that year passed, one proponent of this theory was asked what happened in 1994 that fulfilled his predictions. At least he was honest enough to acknowledge that nothing had happened—*that you could see.*

New Agers, many of whom make no profession of being Bible students, claim that the world has entered the Age of Aquarius and predict great changes based on astrology. Some of these believe that the rapid changes taking place in the world are signs that the world stands on the verge of a new world order.

As the year 2000 approaches, the voices of some Christians are heard suggesting that Jesus may come or even will come in that year. They base their belief on the assumption that the year 2000 will mark the end of the sixth millennium and that the world will see the nations fight the Battle of Armageddon.

SDAs Not the Only Newspaper Prophets

Adventists are not the only Christians in recent years who have made predictions that have not come to pass. In his book, *Chariots of Salvation,* Hans K. La Rondelle calls attention to the fact that

> Popular religious writers point especially to the Armageddon prophecy of the last Bible book (Rev. 16:16). They argue that this prophecy refers to the territory of the Megiddo Valley, near Mount Carmel in northern Palestine, as the battleground for the final war. . . .
>
> The literalists, who refer to themselves as dispensationalists, consider the year 1948 as the beginning of the final generation of the Israel of God. They appeal to Christ's statement to His disciples, "This generation will certainly not pass away until all these things have happened" (Mark 13:30). Taking the duration of a "generation" as 40 years, many concluded that the year 1988 would be the year of "Armageddon." Hal Lindsey wrote in his best-seller *The Late Great Planet Earth* (New York: Bantam Books, 1973):
>
>> What generation? Obviously, in the context, the generation that would see the signs—chief among them the rebirth of Israel. A generation in the Bible is something like forty years. If this is a correct de-

duction, then within forty years or so from 1948, all these things could take place (p. 54).

We are the generation He was talking about! (*The 1980s Countdown to Armageddon* [New York: Bantam Books, 1982], p. 162).

In keeping with this calculation, some reckoned that their rapture to heaven would take place seven years before 1988 and actually prepared for their liftoff from earth in 1981.[3]

An attack on Israel by the Soviet Union or Russia figured prominently in the initial stages of Lindsey's countdown. Unfortunately, he didn't foresee that just a year after Christ's supposed return in 1988, the Soviet Union would begin to collapse and the chances that it, or Russia, would invade Israel would become quite remote.

Other Evangelicals have been even more positive in their predictions. Robert P. Lightner points out that Edgar C. Whisenant in his book, *88 Reasons Why the Rapture Could Be in 1988* claimed "with considerable boasting that he had incontrovertible proof that his date for Christ's return in 1988 was correct and, only if the Bible was wrong, could he be wrong. When it became obvious he *was* wrong, he changed the date to January 1989 and later updated it again to September 1989."[4]

Such prognosticating is reminiscent of the fabled sheepherder who cried, "Wolf! Wolf!" too many times and lost his credibility.[5]

SDAs, Not Prophets, but Proclaimers of the Sure Word of Prophecy

All predictions that Christ will return in a certain year or that certain eschatological events will take place on certain dates are *not* the sure word of prophecy. The writings of Ellen White repeatedly caution Seventh-day Adventists against making such predictions. In 1892 she wrote:

> Again and again I have been warned in regard to time-setting. There will never again [since October 22, 1844] be a message for the people of God that will be based on time.[6]

Numerous other statements could be cited to the same effect. Adventists were not raised up to be prophets. We have been called, we believe, to be proclaimers of the "sure word of prophecy" (2 Pet. 1:19)—*and there is a distinct difference between the two*. When a Bible writer or the Spirit of Prophecy clearly predict that a certain apocalyptic event will occur, we can rest assured that the event will take place as predicted, but we are to set no dates for it to happen, nor should we go any further than the sure word of prophecy warrants. The Bible and the Spirit of Prophecy writings give us many cause-and-effect links between events that are to occur in the future, but how much time elapses between the present and those events, or between one future event and the next, is not revealed. (See the author's *The Shape of the Coming Crisis,* published by Pacific Press® Publishing Association, Copyright © 1998, and available in your ABC.) Because this is true, we are encouraged to carefully and prayerfully keep our spiritual ears to the ground, catching what Ellen White calls "the steady tread of events,"[7] all the while guarding against the temptation to be prophets.

Because "the final movements will be rapid ones,"[8] all of us may be taken by surprise by the rapidity with which events foretold will unfold, hence the need to be vigilant at all times. Christ could come *before* the year 2000, for "the end will come more quickly than men expect."[9] On the other hand, Christ may "tarry" (Matt. 25:5) beyond 2000. The important thing is to be ready and realize that the signs of His coming indicate He "is near, even at the doors" (Matt. 24:33).

Why God Predicts the Future

God's primary purpose in foretelling the future and giving signs of the nearness of the coming of Christ is not that we might know the "day and hour" of Jesus' coming (Matt. 24:36; 25:13; Acts 1:6, 7) or the specific time when some eschatological event will occur (1 Thess. 5:1, 2) but that when the "sure word of prophecy" (2 Pet. 1:19), as revealed by the signs given by the inspired writers, comes to pass, we "may believe" (John 13:19). In other words, the purpose of prophecy is not to make us prophets but to strengthen our faith when we see the things predicted happening.

---

1. Robert P. Lightner, *The Last Days Handbook* (Nashville: Thomas Nelson Publishers, 1990), pp. 68, 69.
2. Richard Lewinsohn, *Science, Prophecy and Prediction* (New York: Bell, 1961), p. 78.
3. Hans K. La Rondelle, *Chariots of Salvation* (Hagerstown, Md: Review and Herald Publishing Association, 1987), p. 14.
4. Lightner, p. 172.
5. "Some have set a time [for the Second Coming], and when that has passed, their presumptuous spirits have not accepted rebuke, but they have set another and another time; but many successive failures have stamped them as false prophets" (*Fundamentals of Christian Education*, p. 335).
6. *The Advent Review and Sabbath Herald* (abbreviated *Review* in the text and *RH* in footnotes). See also *RH,* October 9, 1894, and March 22, 1892.
7. Ellen G. White, *Testimonies for the Church* (Nampa, Idaho: Pacific Press® Publishing Association, 1948), vol. 7, p. 14. *Testimonies for the Church,* abbrev., *7T,* p. 14; *1T* through *9T.*
8. *9T, p.* 11.
9. Ellen G. White, *Spirit of Prophecy* (Battle Creek, Mich.: Steam Press of the Seventh-day Adventist Publishing Association, 1878), vol. 4, p. 447. abbrev., *4SP,* p. 447; *1SP* through *4SP.*

CHAPTER
Two

WORLD WAR I
AND
ARMAGEDDON

Early on the morning of August 5, 1914, a young clerk working in a tobacco shop in New York City arrived at his place of employment and began setting out the daily papers. As he ripped off the wrapper from a bundle of the *New York Times*, he was stunned by the headline that leapt out at him. It consisted of a single word in the largest black type available and read—
ARMAGEDDON!

One doesn't have to be a student of Bible prophecy to sense that the word *Armageddon* sounds ominous. To many minds, even secular minds, it conjures up visions of armed conflict of cataclysmic proportions.

The young tobacconist was more familiar with the biblical meaning of Armageddon than his average customer. A third-generation Adventist, he had served as tent master to Evangelist J. W. Lair, in Parkersburg, West Virginia, during the latter weeks of the Russo-Japanese War of 1904–05. The young teenager had listened to evangelist Lair's description of the horrendous carnage associated with Armageddon, and it left an indelible impression on his mind. Yet, strange to say, only a few days after the signing of the Treaty of Portsmouth, ending the Russo-Japanese War, the teenager ran away from home, joined an older brother who worked as an artist in New York City, and took up the ways of the world. The Russo-Japanese War had not developed into Armageddon as Pastor Lair had predicted, and the teenager was sure he had many more years to get ready for the Second Coming.

After a couple of years of working as an artist, the young man took a job as a clerk in a tobacco shop near the Bowery, where he lived. About the time he thought he had forgotten everything Evangelist Lair had preached about, he had a terrifying dream. He dreamed about Armageddon and the end of the world. So it is not surprising that the headline that stared the young clerk in the face that August morning in 1914 brought back memories of the final, cataclysmic battle of nations—cavalrymen charging into battle through gore that came up to the horses' bridles (Rev. 14:20). In fact, the young prodigal later confessed that three times during those ten years he dreamed the same horrific dream—and *he was a participant in the battle*. He invariably woke up in a cold sweat.

That young clerk was my father.[1]

The Prodigal Son Returns Home

A short time prior to the outbreak of the war, my father began corresponding with his half sister, Lillian. One day, not long after the headline in the *New York Times*, she wrote and said she smelled tobacco on his letters and asked if he smoked. He wrote back and admitted he did. He said he had tried to quit many times but couldn't break the habit.

Aunt Lillian pleaded for him to quit smoking and come home to Huntington, West Virginia, where his father's family was now living. After several more letters, she succeeded in persuading him to quit his job and return to his father's house.[2]

When the prodigal arrived in Huntington, Evangelist Charles T. Redfield was in the midst of a series of evangelistic lectures on Bible prophecy. By that time, Turkey had entered the war on the side of the Central Powers and the big concern in the minds, not only of Adventists but of other Christians and even secular people was: Is this Armageddon?[3] After all, the world had never seen a war of such gigantic proportions.

Adventist evangelists took full advantage of this popular concern, and Pastor Redfield was no exception. He always came to his meetings with a sheaf of clippings gleaned from the daily papers and pointed out to his listeners how the happenings in war-torn Europe were fulfilling Bible prophecy. He frequently quoted British Prime Minister Henry H. Asquith's prediction that by entering the conflict on the side of the Central Powers, Turkey had "rung her death knell."[4]

The war, Evangelist Redfield stated with great positiveness, would see Turkey driven from Europe. Before long the Turk would set up "the tabernacles of its palace" in Jerusalem—"the glorious holy mountain" between the Mediterranean Sea and Dead Sea—and there would come to his ignominious end, and no nation would lift a finger to help the infidel. This, the evangelist told his audience, was predicted by the prophecy of Daniel 11:45. But this wasn't all.

Following the exodus of the "sick man of the East,"[5] the Turk would set up his capital at Jerusalem. The jealousies of the European powers would cause them to send armies to Palestine to protect the holy sepulchers. Once there, they would wipe Turkey off the map. Just how the warring armies on the Western

Front would disengage, unite in common cause against Turkey—one of the allies of the Central Powers—transfer their forces to Palestine and destroy Turkey, he didn't explain.

Somehow the destruction of the Turkish nation would be the signal for "the kings of the east" (Rev. 16:12)—the nations of Asia—to move westward. After crossing the Euphrates River and arriving in Palestine, there would be a falling out among the armies and the bloodiest battle in the history of humankind would be fought at Megiddo—the Armageddon of Revelation 16:13, 14, and 16.

In the midst of the battle Christ would suddenly appear and annihilate not only the warring combatants but the rest of the wicked as well. He would then resurrect the righteous dead and take them, together with the righteous living, to heaven (1 Thess. 4:16, 17; John 14:1-3; Heb. 11:13-16), where they would spend the next thousand years before returning to the earth.

The graphic scenario presented was convincing. After all, hadn't Christ prophesied that there would be wars and rumors of wars; that nation would "rise against nation, and kingdom against kingdom" (Matt. 24:6, 7)? Weren't men's hearts figuratively failing them for fear, and for looking after those things that were coming on the earth (Luke 21:26)? Look at the incidence of heart failure. Hadn't Joel prophesied there shall be "blood and fire, and pillars of smoke" (Joel 2:30)? Look at the terrible fires resulting from the razing of cities in Belgium and France. Look at the increasing interest in spiritism resulting from the deaths of thousands of young men on the fields of Flanders. Hadn't John the revelator seen "three unclean spirits, like frogs," going forth to gather "the kings of the earth" to the battle of Armageddon? Hadn't British statesman Sir Edward Grey said that it seemed "as if in the atmosphere of our world" the spirits of devils were inciting the nations to go to war?

The lectures were gripping, and scores requested baptism, convinced that the world stood "at Armageddon."[6] My father was one of them. With God's help he gave up tobacco and remained a loyal Adventist for the rest of his life.[7] In fact, he became a minister, and I, as a boy growing up, remember him holding evangelistic meetings and preaching about the coming battle of Armageddon.

At these meetings it was my job to run my father's slide projector. Two slides he used to illustrate his lectures left an indelible impression. The first was a cartoon showing eight or ten caricatures—the leading nations of the world—lined up singing. The caption read, "Peace, Peace, Wonderful Peace." On the first slide the nations faced the audience. On the left was a rotund John Bull, next to him a tall, lanky Uncle Sam, and on the extreme right stood little Japan on a soap box, displaying a toothy grin.

The next slide showed a rear view of the same group. Each held in his right hand a cocked pistol. The caption again read, "Peace, Peace, Wonderful Peace."

In Spite of Faulty Methods God Overrules for the Good

Not everyone who joined the Adventist Church through our preaching on the Eastern Question and Armageddon during World War I stayed in the church. When events didn't materialize as confidently predicted, large numbers of disillusioned converts left the church.

Despite the fact that predictions of our Adventist evangelists failed, I thank God that my father was impressed by the preaching of Elders Lair and Redfield, rejoined the church, and remained faithful to the Adventist message. But simply because God overruled in his case, and in the case of others, is not a good reason why Seventh-day Adventists should win souls by setting times or making eschatological predictions that are not part of the sure word of prophecy.

---

1. From the unpublished "The Memoirs of Ernest P. Mansell" and the author's conversations with him.
2. Ibid., as well as conversations with my Aunt Lillian.
3. Ibid.
4. John E. Fulton, *Signs of the Times,* Aug. 17, 1915. Abbrev. *ST.*
5. A term coined by Chancellor Otto von Bismarck in the 1870s.
6. Theodore Roosevelt's slogan for his 1912 presidential campaign: "We stand at Armageddon and we battle for the Lord."
7. From the "Memoirs of Ernest P. Mansell" and the author's conversations with him.

CHAPTER
THREE

EARLY ADVENTIST VIEWS

From time to time, long-standing tensions in the Middle East erupt into armed conflict, leading some Bible students to predict that the world is on the verge of Armageddon. This battle is supposed to center at Megiddo in Palestine, from which, it is believed, its name is derived. Here, according to some students of Bible prophecy, the most horrific of all wars will be fought. In the past many Seventh-day Adventists subscribed to this interpretation of Revelation 16:12-16.

One thing seems certain: Regardless of differences of interpretation, virtually all Adventists agree that one's view of Armageddon and the last power of Daniel 11 (see Dan. 11:40-45), which has frequently been linked with it, is not a matter of salvation. Yet these differences have occasioned some of the sharpest and bitterest disagreements that have ever arisen among our people.

For instance, on September 28, 1878, James White, then General Conference president, publicly confronted Uriah

Smith, editor of the church paper the *Review,* during the camp meeting that preceded the General Conference session, over Smith's identification of the last power of Daniel 11.[1]

In 1920 William T. Bartlett was replaced by Arthur S. Maxwell as editor of the British *Present Truth* and "exiled" to the mission field because he disagreed with the then generally accepted view of the last power of Daniel 11.[2]

In the early 40s, two teachers in one of our senior colleges engaged in a "battle" of push and shove over differences in their interpretations of Armageddon and the king of the north.[3]

As late as 1959, a group of ministers on a tour of the Bible lands "warmly" discussed the question of Armageddon as they stood on the ruins of old Megiddo. Some contended that this was where the world's last and greatest war would be fought. Others insisted that the Valley of Megiddo, even including the surrounding area, was too small to accommodate all the armies of the world. The debate, predictably, generated more heat than light.[4]

An Outline of Adventist Teachings on the Eastern Question

In view of the fact that one's interpretation of Armageddon and the king of the north, often called "The Eastern Question," is not a matter of salvation, the question arises: Why discuss the matter at all? The answer is that, by reviewing our past teachings on the matter, we may avoid unnecessary conflicts in the future as well as the risk of embarrassing ourselves by making predictions that fail.

The chart on the following page illustrates the changes that have occurred in our teachings on Armageddon and the king of the north during the course of the history of our church.

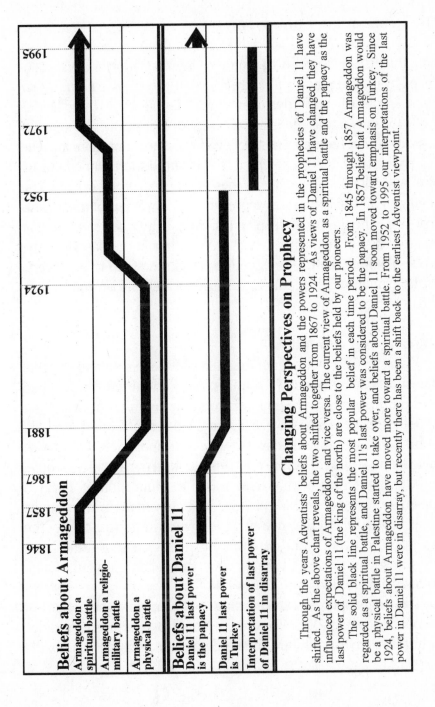

Beliefs about Armageddon

Armageddon a spiritual battle

Armageddon a religio-military battle

Armageddon a physical battle

Beliefs about Daniel 11

Daniel 11 last power is the papacy

Daniel 11 last power is Turkey

Interpretation of last power of Daniel 11 in disarray

1846 · 1857 · 1867 · 1881 · 1924 · 1952 · 1972 · 1995

Changing Perspectives on Prophecy

Through the years Adventists' beliefs about Armageddon and the powers represented in the prophecies of Daniel 11 have shifted. As the above chart reveals, the two shifted together from 1867 to 1924. As views of Daniel 11 have changed, they have influenced expectations of Armageddon, and vice versa. The current view of Armageddon as a spiritual battle and the papacy as the last power of Daniel 11 (the king of the north) are close to the beliefs held by our pioneers.

The solid black line represents the most popular belief in each time period. From 1845 through 1857 Armageddon was regarded as a spiritual battle, and Daniel 11's last power was considered to be the papacy. In 1857 belief that Armageddon would be a physical battle in Palestine started to take over, and beliefs about Daniel 11 soon moved toward emphasis on Turkey. Since 1924, beliefs about Armageddon have moved more toward a spiritual battle. From 1952 to 1995 our interpretations of the last power in Daniel 11 were in disarray, but recently there has been a shift back to the earliest Adventist viewpoint.

23

The Roots of the Controversy

Seventh-day Adventism did not originate in a vacuum. It arose from the historical school of prophetic interpretation and was influenced by it. An analysis of LeRoy E. Froom's *Prophetic Faith of Our Fathers,* vols. III and IV, dealing with Revelation 16:12-16 and Daniel 11:40-45, shows that the great majority of William Miller's predecessors and contemporaries believed that the Euphrates and the last power of Daniel 11 referred to the Turco-Mohammedan Empire. A small minority believed these to represent the papacy. The drying up of the Euphrates represented the waning of these powers. As for the timing of the plagues, the majority believed them to be great historical events, which were either in the past or in the process of fulfillment. Armageddon was understood to be a literal battle, usually in the Middle East, during which Christ would come and destroy the warring nations.

Millerite Interpretations

William Miller, founder of the Millerite Movement and spiritual ancestor of Seventh-day Adventists, was undoubtedly influenced by the milieu of prophetic interpretation in which he lived, yet he held some views that were distinctly different from those held by his Protestant predecessors and contemporaries. Along with them he believed the Euphrates represented the Turkish people, and the drying up of this river was the diminution of Turkish power. As for the seven last plagues, he believed these were seven great historical events, five of which were in the past, one, the drying up of the Euphrates, was in the process of fulfillment, and the seventh would take place at the second advent, which he believed would occur in 1843–44.

The kings of the east, according to Miller, were the nations of Europe. Under the sixth plague, these "kings" would invade America with their armies and fight the battle of Armageddon. The battle would be primarily military but would have religious overtones. In the midst of the battle Christ would suddenly appear, defeat His enemies, and save His people.[5] In later years Miller altered his view on some of these points.[6]

Miller believed the king of the north to be the papacy.[7]

Although most of the Millerites agreed with Miller's views, some did not. A few followed the teachings of Josiah Litch, one of Miller's chief lieutenants. According to Litch, Christ would come and take (rapture?) His people to the sea of glass (not heaven), where He would organize His kingdom. Meanwhile the plagues would be falling. Under the sixth vial Christ would come with His saints, fight the battle of Armageddon at Jerusalem, and drive out the wicked from the Holy City. The Euphrates, he held, represented the literal river.[8] Thus he believed that the plagues would fall *after* the Second Coming.[9] According to Litch, Napoleon Bonaparte was the last power of Daniel 11.

Interpretations After the Disappointment

Interpretations concerning Armageddon and the king of the north were, understandably, not major concerns of the Millerites immediately after the Great Disappointment of October 22, 1844. Records for the following five or six years are scanty, but those that survive show that interpretations shifted radically and erratically during those years.

As early as August 1847, Joseph Bates, one of the founders of the Seventh-day Adventist Church, believed that the seven last plagues would be poured out in the future, *after* the proclamation of the third angel's message calling God's people out of Babylon—the apostate churches.[10] In 1849 he believed that "a part of the 144,000 will come from" Asia and that when the "sixth seal [vial?]" is poured out, "the river Euphrates will be dried up before them to cross over . . . 'in THE GREAT

DAY OF THE LORD.' "[11]

By April of the next year Bates had adopted a view that came closer to the position adopted by the Sabbath-keeping Adventists for the next twenty years. He is quoted as teaching

> that the seven last plagues are all in the future, which will be a time of trouble, when God will speak, fulfilling Hag. 2:6, 21; that this is the signal for the great battle of God; that the 144,000 sealed (Rev. 14:1) are all the living saints who are sealed by receiving his [Bates's] message, whose sins are blotted out, and who [are to] have power over the nations, to execute the judgment written, Ps. 149:9; that then the battle commences, in which the wicked are nearly or quite all slain.[12]

Hiram Edson's Changing Views

Hiram Edson, the Adventist pioneer who first realized that Christ had entered the most holy place in the heavenly sanctuary on October 22, 1844, believed in the late 1840s and up to the fall of 1850 that the Jews would return to Jerusalem. While there, Armageddon would be fought, in which Russia, the king of the north, would be involved.[13]

This view of Armageddon and the king of the north never gained many followers, and by September of 1850 Edson had abandoned it and begun emphasizing that Armageddon would be a battle over the Sabbath question.[14]

James White's Views

Just what James White, the young Millerite preacher who later became one of the founders of the Seventh-day Adventist Church, believed with respect to Armageddon and the last power of Daniel 11 before the Great Disappointment is not known. He probably held the generally accepted Millerite view that this power was the papacy, but this is by no means certain.

What is known for sure is that about May 1846 he changed his view on the timing of the plagues; for, in *A Word to the Little Flock* (abbrev. *WLF*, dated May 30, 1847), the first publication of the Sabbath-keeping Adventists, he says on the first page of the brochure that "for about a year" he had believed that the plagues were all in the *future*, but *before* the Second Coming. This view clearly differed from Miller's interpretation as well as Litch's view. But more importantly, White's interpretation remains the Adventist position on the timing of the plagues to this day.

Why did White, Bates, and others change their views? We cannot be dogmatic, but it is almost certain that the visions of Ellen Harmon, who married White on August 30, 1846, had something to do with it. For example, in *WLF*, p. 22, James states that in the summer of 1845 he and Ellen thought a mistake of a year had been made in calculating the end of the 2,300 days and that Christ would come in October 1845. However, in a vision Ellen had a few weeks before,[15] she saw that they would be again disappointed, for they must yet go through "the time of Jacob's trouble." The time of Jacob's trouble was an entirely new concept for the young couple, and it altered their understanding of end-time events.

Armageddon, a Battle Over the Sabbath Question

As James White's interpretations of prophecy developed, he came to believe that the battle of Armageddon was the climactic clash between the forces of good and evil, culminating at the Second Advent, and that the seventh-day Sabbath was the great point at issue. Others quickly followed his lead, among them such early leaders as Joseph Bates, John Nevins Andrews, Hiram Edson, Roswell F. Cottrell, David Arnold, George W. Holt, and others.

The Rise of Spiritism and Armageddon

Modern spiritualism (spiritism is a better term, for there is nothing particularly "spiritual" about spiritualism) arose in Hydesville, New York, in March 1848, when Margaret and Kate Fox began communicating with the supposed spirit of John Rosma, a murdered peddler, by means of rapping noises. A few months later, they visited their sister, Leah Fish, in Rochester, New York, and exhibited their mysterious powers at the Corinthian Hall before an audience that paid "rapt" attention to their eerie way of communicating with the deceased. From Rochester, the phenomenon spread like wildfire and became known as the "Rochester Rappings."

On August 24, 1850, Ellen White was shown in vision that the "spirit rappings that had just commenced in Rochester"[16] were caused by "the power of Satan."[17] She was also informed that " 'the rapping . . . would spread more and more.' "[18]

Before long, leaders of the Sabbath-keeping Adventists began identifying the spirits of spiritism with the "spirits of devils, working miracles, which go forth unto the kings of the earth and of the whole world, to gather them to the battle of that great day of God Almighty" (Rev. 16:14). Thus, in 1851 James White stated that "the 'foul spirits' that Babylon was to become the 'hold' of, . . . refers to the spiritual wonders of the present day, such as . . . the 'Mysterious Rappings.' "[19] In time he identified these spirits as the agents that gather the nations to "the battle of the great day of God Almighty."[20]

A few months earlier George W. Holt, a frequent contributor to the *Review,* said, after quoting Revelation 16:13, 14:

> This undoubtedly is the work of Sorcery practiced by many at the present time, by the deceptive arts under the names of Biology, Psychology, Mesmerism, and spiritual

rappings, or pretended communication with the dead. John does not say that this work of deception commenced with the pouring out of the sixth vial; but he here has another view and saw by what *means* the wicked would be gathered together to the great battle.[21]

Samuel W. Rhodes, a Millerite preacher who joined the Sabbath-keeping Adventists, identified "rapology" as the work of "those 'spirits of devils' " that would be involved "in the last, mighty conflict."[22] David Arnold declared that "Satan with his legions of fallen angels, or spirits of Devils [*sic*], is working through Psychology, Mesmerism, and the so-called spirit manifestation, to 'deceive the whole world.' "[23] E. R. Seaman, a contributor to the church paper, wrote that Adventists had "no fellowship with the" " 'Rapping Spirits' " but believed "them to be the spirits of devils working miracles, which are gathering the whole world to the last mighty and final conflict."[24]

From this time on Seventh-day Adventists have believed that the gathering of the nations to Armageddon will be accomplished by "the spirits of devils" working through spiritism, regardless of the nature of the battle or the issues involved.

---

1. *Review and Herald,* October 3, 1878, abbrev. *RH,* Oct. 3, 1878.
2. Statement of S. Lawrence Maxwell to the author.
3. A. Graham Maxwell on his tape, "Christ for Time and Eternity," (C) & (P), Revelation I, May 6, 1989, side 2, says: "I think of two saints who used to . . . We [might say?] they even came to physical contact on the steps of Irwin Hall at P.U.C. over the matter of Armageddon. We almost saw it [the battle] start right there on the steps." Leo R. Van Dolson, at the time a student at Pacific Union College, witnessed this altercation and told this author it was a battle of "push and shove."

In 1951 this author asked one of the "combatants" if it was true that he and another teacher had gotten "physical" over Armageddon, and he admitted, "Yes, to our shame, it is true."

4. Reminisces of the author.

5. William Miller, *Evidence From Scirpture [Scripture] and History of the Second Coming of Christ About the Year 1843* (Troy: Kemble and Hooper, 1836), pp. 208-210, 218-220.

6. *The Western Midnight Cry,* Mar. 4, 1844, p. 104; *The Advent Herald and Signs of the Times Reporter,* Oct. 16, 1844, p. 88, e.g., Armageddon is the "place [where] Christ will gather his elect" at His second coming, and was interpreted to mean *"the mountain of the gospel,* or otherwise, *the mountain of fruits."*

7. *Evidences . . . ,* pp. 95, 96.

8. Ibid., vol. 1, pp. 175, 180-183, 189-192.

9. *Prophetic Expositions; or a Connected View of the Testimony of the Prophets Concerning the Kingdom of God and the Time of Its Establishment* (Boston, Mass.: Joshua V. Himes, 1842), vol. 1, p. 175.

10. Joseph Bates, *Second Advent Waymarks and High Heaps, or a Connected View, of the Fulfilment of Prophecy by God's Peculiar People* (New Bedford: Press of Benjamin Lindsey, 1847), p. 20.

11. Joseph Bates, *A Seal of the Living God. A Hundred Forty-Four Thousand, of the Servants of God Being Sealed, in 1849* (New Bedford: Press of Benjamin Lindsey, 1849), p. 62. See also pp. 15, 25, 26, 45, 49, 51, 53 (for his concept of the standing up of Michael and the time of trouble); p. 37 (for his concept of the coming Sunday vs. Sabbath conflict); p. 47 (for his concept of the seven last plagues).

12. M. L. Clark in *The Advent Herald* (Boston), vol. 5 (May 4, 1850), pp. 110, 111.

13. Hiram Edson, *An Exposition of Scripture Prophecy; Showing the Final Return of the Jews in 1850* (Canandaigua, N.Y.: Office of the Ontario Messenger, 1849), pp. 1, 10, 13, 28-30, 32.

14. *RH, Extra,* Sept. 1850, pp. 12, 13.

15. *WLF,* p. 22: "It is well known that many were expecting the Lord to come at the 7th month [October] 1845. That Christ would then come we firmly believed. A few days before the time passed, I was at Fairhaven, and Dartmouth[,] Mass., with a message on this point of time. At this time, Ellen [G. Harmon] was with the band in Carver, Mass., where she saw in vision, that we should be disappointed, and that the saints must pass through the 'time of Jacob's trouble,' which was future. Her view of Jacob's trouble was entirely new to us, as well as to herself." See also Bates's *A Seal of the Living God . . . ,* p. 24, where he says: "I had believed that this *ascending* [of the sealing angel of Rev. 7:2] was to have been taken in a literal sense, . . . but God in answer to united prayer gave us clear light upon it, through sister Ellen G. White."

16. Ellen G. White, *Spiritual Gifts* (Battle Creek, Mich.: James White Publisher, 1880), vol. 2, p. 142. Abbrev. *2SG,* p.142; *1SG* through *4bSG.*

17. Ellen G. White, *Early Writings* (Washington, D.C.: Review and Herald Publishing Association, 1882, 1945), p. 59. abbrev. *EW.*

18. Ibid., pp. 86, 87.

19. *The Advent Review and Sabbath Herald,* Dec. 9, 1951; abbrev. *RH,* and abbrev. *Review* in the body of the text.

20. *RH,* June 24, 1852.

21. *RH,* Mar. 23, 1852. "Biology," as defined by *The Oxford Dictionary* (1933 ed.) at one time meant " 'animal magnetism,' a phase of mesmerism." *The Century Dictionary and Cyclopedia* (1901 ed.) defines "to psychologize" as "to hypnotize or mesmerize." It seems that Holt was lumping the various forms of hypnotism under the umbrella of spirit phenomena.

22. *RH,* Oct. 28, 1852.

23. *RH,* July 21, 1853.

24. *RH,* Nov. 1, 1853.

FOUR

URIAH SMITH'S CHANGING VIEWS OF ESCHATOLOGY

Uriah Smith joined the *Review and Herald* staff early in 1853. For the next three or four years he held eschatological views virtually identical to those held by James White and the other Adventist leaders.[1] This is clearly demonstrated by a lengthy poem he wrote, which was published in the church paper.[2] However, by mid-1857, Smith's view of eschatology had begun to shift from his original interpretation, apparently influenced by currently popular futuristic views of Armageddon.

Smith now began to express the belief that the Euphrates symbolized the Turkish Empire and that Armageddon was a war of nations. In adopting this view, he frankly admitted that "the view we may take may differ from some; [and] many it may not help."[3] Smith did not at this time say where the battle would be fought. However, others who adopted his new interpretation did. Thus, Otis Nichols, in the *Review* of July 7, 1859, and R. Baker, in the *Review* of July 2, 1861, stated that the battle would be fought in the "valley of Jehoshaphat," near Jerusalem.

A few months after Baker's article, James White reacted vigorously against the view that Armageddon would be fought in Palestine. In the *Review* of January 21, 1862, he stated unequivocally that "the great battle is not between nation and nation; but between earth and heaven," during which the nations are destroyed by the "terrible burning glory" of the Second Advent. "As to the place of gathering," he wrote, "we only wish to say at this time that we think there are good reasons to locate it where Christ makes his descent at his second coming." Because this is the only time White set forth his view of Armageddon in any great detail, we here reproduce the portions that are significant:

> In view of the civil war of the States, and the warlike attitude of other nations, the question is sometimes asked, "Is not the battle of that great day of God Almighty commencing?" We wish to offer a few thoughts upon the battle of that great day, which may lead to a more thorough investigation, and a better understanding of this subject.
>
> We have probably entered but the threshold of our own national difficulties [the Civil War, 1861–1865, was raging]. American soil may yet be drenched with human blood. Evil may go forth from nation to nation, and a great whirlwind be raised up from the coasts of the earth, till all nations become imbrued in the horrors of war, yet in all this we do not see the battle of that great day of God Almighty. The special preparations for that battle do not commence until the time of the pouring out of the sixth vial. [Rev. 16:12-14, quoted.]

It is evident from what White says that many Adventists believed that the American Civil War was the beginning of Arma-

33

geddon and that he wished to dispel this notion. White continues:

The spirits of devils are now being manifested in what is called Spiritualism, which is filling the world with skepticism in reference to the sacred Scriptures; but the time for them to "go forth" to gather the kings of the earth and the whole world to the battle of that great day is yet future. As to the place of gathering, we only wish to say at this time that we think there are good reasons to locate it where Christ makes his descent at his second coming.

"And I saw heaven opened, and behold a white horse; and he that sat upon him was called Faithful and True, and in righteousness he doth judge and make war. His eyes were as a flame of fire, and on his head were many crowns; and he had a name written, that no man knew, but he himself. And he was clothed in a vesture dipped in blood: and his name is called, The Word of God. And the armies which were in heaven followed him upon white horses, clothed in fine linen, white and clean." Rev. xix, 11-14.

The person described is the Son of God. The armies of heaven which followed him are the angels. An army of horsemen is here used to represent the majestic approach of Christ to this earth, accompanied by the host of heaven.

Verses 15, 16. "And out of his mouth goeth a sharp sword, that with it he should smite the nations: and he shall rule them with a rod of iron: and he treadeth the winepress of the fierceness and wrath of Almighty God." . . .

Compare with this, Chap. xvii, 13, 14. "These have one mind, and shall give their power and strength unto the beast. These shall make war with the Lamb, and the Lamb shall overcome them; for he is Lord of lords, and King of kings; and they that are with him are called, and chosen, and faithful."

34

Here, then, the great battle is fought, and there is no proof that a gun is to be fired. The power by which Christ and his army overcome is represented by a sharp sword going out of the great Leader's mouth. This power is also spoken of in 2 Thess. ii, 8: "Whom the Lord shall consume with the Spirit of his mouth, and shall destroy with the brightness of his coming." Again, Chap. i, 7, 8: "When the Lord Jesus shall be revealed from heaven with his mighty angels, in *flaming fire,* taking vengeance on them that know not God, and that obey not the gospel of our Lord Jesus Christ." This last quotation does not say the world will be set on fire when Jesus is revealed from heaven; but it declares that Jesus and the mighty angels will be revealed in flaming fire, which fire, we understand represents the dreadful burning glory of an angry God which attends the army of heaven. Here is unquenchable fire.

Verses 17, 18 [of Rev. xix, say:] "And I saw an angel standing in the sun; and he cried with a loud voice, saying to all the fowls that fly in the midst of heaven, Come and gather yourselves together unto the supper of the great God; That ye may eat the flesh of kings, and the flesh of captains, and the flesh of mighty men, and the flesh of horses, and of them that sit on them, and the flesh of all men, both free and bond, both small and great." . . .

Here it is seen that the great battle is not between nation and nation; but between earth and heaven. Satan wishes to make another attack on Jesus Christ. He musters the fallen spirits of his command, and they go forth to the kings of the earth, and the whole world, to gather them to battle. The King of kings overcomes, and destroys all his enemies.

In White's view Armageddon was clearly not an armed conflict of nations somewhere in Palestine that would be interrupted by the second coming of Christ but the destruction of the forces of evil by Christ and his celestial army at the Second Coming.

The Origin of "D & R"

In the early 1860s, Uriah Smith was a Sabbath School teacher in the Adventist Church in Battle Creek, and James White was one of his pupils. On Sabbath, May 17, 1862, the class began a verse-by-verse study of the book of Revelation. White, at the time editor of the church paper, reported that "all . . . [came] to almost the same conclusion on almost every point."[4]

Because of this near unanimity of opinion, White began publishing a verse-by-verse commentary on Revelation based on Smith's lessons. However, by the time White reached chapters 8 and 9, his articles were becoming increasingly sketchy.[5] The burdens of church leadership during the American Civil War, traveling among the churches, and editing the *Review* were occupying too much of his time, making it difficult for him to continue. He asked Smith to take over the responsibility of continuing with his comments in the church paper. Smith "consented to conclude the book, commencing with chapter X."[6]

In the light of later developments, it would be interesting to know how White would have reacted when Smith reached Revelation 16:12-16[7] if he had been less preoccupied with other matters. As editor of the *Review,* would he have let Smith present in the church paper an interpretation that was substantially different from the view most Adventists espoused? We shall never know. What we do know is that when Smith reached Revelation 16, he said "he inclined to the . . . opinion" that the Euphrates symbolized "the nation occupying the territory through which . . . [that river] flows," in other words, "the Ottoman or Turkish empire," and he believed that Armageddon would be "fought" at

"Jerusalem."[8] This, apparently, was the first time Smith publicly pinpointed the place where the battle would be fought. The Valley of Jehoshaphat lies between Jerusalem and the Mount of Olives.

Smith concluded his commentary on Revelation in the *Review* of Febuary 3, 1863. His treatment of the book was so popular with readers of the church paper that he was urged to publish his articles in book form. His book, *Thoughts . . . on the Book of Revelation,* came off the press about May 1867, although the title page bears the date 1865. Apparently Smith was perfecting his comments during this interval. Whatever the case, soon after the book began to circulate, he was encouraged to write a commentary on the book of Daniel and agreed to undertake this task.

Shift in Interpretation of Daniel 11:45

There is undeniable evidence that from the mid-1850s and up to late 1867 most SDAs, including Smith, believed that the papacy was the last power of Daniel 11. For instance, in the *Review* of May 13, 1862, under the initials "U.S.," Smith, quoting the *Liverpool Mercury,* which spoke of the "removing of the seat of the Papacy to Jerusalem," asked approvingly if this was not "significant, taken in connection with Dan. xi, 45?"[9] Other unsigned editorials, probably written by Smith, who some of this time was "Resident Editor," express the same view. (See endnote 9.) But by the fall of 1867, we begin to detect a shift away from this generally accepted Adventist view.

In the *Review* of Nov. 5, 1867, while working on his weekly comments on Daniel, Smith suggested that another interpretation of Daniel 11:45 was possible. His reason for shifting seems clear. He was interpreting the last verses of Daniel 11 in the light of newspaper reports. Writing in this issue of the church paper, he said "Garibaldi [the Italian patriot and soldier] is determined to gain possession of Rome." If this happened, Smith concluded cautiously, "the temporal power [of the papacy], which, if now taken away, will probably never be revived."

It should be noted that the suggestion that the papacy would never be revived went directly contrary to the accepted Adventist view of Revelation 13; namely, that the papacy's deadly wound of 1798 would be healed and that its political power would be restored. Uriah Smith, incidentally, held the view that while the papacy received the deadly wound in 1798, that wound was healed by the election of a new pope in 1800.[10] But, back to the thread we are pursuing.

In order to understand Smith's caution in saying that the papacy would "probably never be revived," one must consider the historical context in which he made this statement. At the time the papacy, as well as the Turkish Empire, were waning powers. "All sides," Smith suggested, "anticipated" "the speedy overthrow of the Papacy and Mohammedanism."[11] However, the fact remained that neither power had yet been overthrown, so he was cautious and allowed that either the papacy or Mohammedanism (Turkey) could fulfill the prophecy of Daniel 11:45.

Up until March 1871, Smith's comments on Daniel had been appearing each week in the *Review* with clocklike regularity. By then he was dealing with the last verses of Daniel 11. In his explanations of these verses he continued to allow two possible interpretations—the last power of Daniel 11 could be the papacy or it could be Turkey. Thus, as he made his closing comments on this chapter, he said, "time will determine the matter."[12]

Then Smith suspended his comments for six weeks, or until the May 16, 1871, issue of the church paper. His reason for so doing appears obvious—he was looking for straws in the wind to guide him in his interpretation of Daniel 11:45–12:1.

These verses speak of a power that will "plant the tabernacles of his palace between the seas in the glorious holy mountain; yet . . . [will] come to his end and none shall help him." The next verse says, "And at that time shall Michael stand up, the great prince which standeth for the children of thy people: and there shall be a time of trouble, such as never was since there was a nation even to that same time."

What was happening in Europe during those six weeks of silence? France, which for many years had been the principle supporter of the papacy, had just lost the Franco-Prussian war. Apparently, the straw Smith was looking for was the signing of the Peace of Frankfurt. This treaty, signed May 10, 1871, ended the war between Prussia and France. When Smith learned the humiliating terms of the treaty, he evidently concluded that since the papacy's chief defender could no longer help the pontiff, the papacy had no future in the fulfillment of the last verses of Daniel 11.

So when Smith resumed his comments on Daniel 12, he said, "when the Turk, driven from Europe, shall hastily make Jerusalem his temporary seat of government. . . , *then*, according to . . . [Dan. 12:1], we look for the standing up of Michael."[13] The die was cast. From this time forward, Turkey was the last power of Daniel 11 in Smith's articles and editorials. The papacy was out of the picture. Hence, it is not surprising that in his 1873 edition of *Thoughts on Daniel,* Smith confidently declared:

The last vestige of temporal power departed [with Garibaldi's capture of Rome in September 1870], nevermore, said [king] Victor Emmanuel [II of Italy], to be restored; and the pope has been virtually a prisoner in his own palace since that time. . . . The last vestige of temporal power was swept from his grasp.[14]

It is in view of this turn of events that Smith states in the *Review* of Febuary 25, 1873, "The long-cherished desire of Russia to obtain possession of Constantinople and European Turkey . . . throws much light on Dan. 11:45." But more on this later.

By 1882, when his commentaries on Daniel and Revelation were combined into one book as *Thoughts on . . . Daniel and the Revelation* (abbrev. *D&R*), and sold to the public as a subscription book, Smith had become positive, one might almost say cavalier, in his identification of Turkey as the last power of Daniel 11. Thus, in the 1881 edition of his *Thoughts on Daniel,* he brushes off the possibility that the last power of Daniel 11 could be the papacy with these words: "The attempt which some make to bring in the papacy here is so evidently wide of the mark that its consideration need not detain us."[15]

In the light of the resurgence of papal power since that time, we now know that it was Smith who was "wide of the mark." In the next chapter we shall go back a few years and pick up the thread of a disagreement that arose between Smith and James White over Smith's identification of Turkey as the last power of Daniel 11 and the great light Smith seemed to see in events unfolding in the Middle East.

---

1. *RH,* June 20, 1854, and Dec. 4, 1855.
2. *RH,* Mar. 17–May 12, 1853.
3. *RH,* June 18, 1857.
4. *RH,* June 3, 1862.
5. *RH,* Sept. 16, 1862.
6. *RH,* Oct. 21, 1862.
7. *RH,* Dec. 2, 1862.
8. Ibid.
9. For other examples of the Resident Editor's identification of the papacy as the king of the north, see *RH,* April 18, 1864, in which he says, "We look for this man of sin [the pope] soon to plant the tabernacles of his palace between the seas in the glorious holy mountain, Jerusalem, and come to his end with none to help him";

ibid., Jan. 6, 1866; ibid., Feb. 20, 1866, says, "It appears that the Pope is about making up his mind to come to his end with none to help him"; *ibid.,* Sept. 11, 1867.

10. *Daniel and Revelation: The Response of History to the Voice of Prophecy[;] A Verse by Verse Study of these Important Books of the Bible* (Mountain View, California: Pacific Press Publishing Association, 1897), p. 564. "The deadly wound was healed when the papacy was re-established . . . by the election of a new pope, March 14, 1800."

11. *RH,* Nov. 5, 1867.

12. *RH,* Mar. 28, 1871.

13. *RH,* Nov. 5, 1871, emphasis his.

14. Uriah Smith, *Thoughts . . . on Daniel* (Battle Creek, Mich.: Review and Herald Steam Press, 1873), pp. 146, 147.

15. *D&R* (1882, ed.), p. 283.

CLASH OVER THE LAST POWER OF DANIEL 11

Having gone through the Great Disappointment of 1844, James White was far more cautious about making predictions concerning future events than was Smith. Thus, White offered words of caution, almost certainly directed at Smith, who had written in the *Review* of March 28, 1871, "All eyes are now turned with interest toward Turkey" and who saw Russia's desire to gain possession of European Turkey and the Dardanelles as throwing "much light on Daniel 11:45."[1]

Here are White's famous words of caution:

There are those who think more of future truth than of present truth. They see but little light in the path in which they walk, but think they see great light ahead of them.

Positions taken on the Eastern Question are based upon prophecies which have not yet [had] their fulfillment. Here we should tread lightly, and take positions carefully, lest we be found removing the landmarks fully established in the advent movement. It may be said that there is a general agreement upon this subject, and that all eyes are turned toward the war now in progress between Turkey and Russia as the fulfillment of that portion of prophecy which will give great confirmation of faith in the soon loud cry and close of our message. But what will be the result of this positiveness in unfulfilled prophecy, should things not come out as very confidently expected, is an anxious question.[2]

These words of caution regarding unfulfilled prophecy were excellent advice then. They are excellent advice today.

Smith reprinted White's *Signs* editorial twelve days later in the November 27, 1877, issue of the *Review.* Several weeks after this, Smith published his reaction to White's words of caution. He protested that he had "ever been careful to guard against the idea that this present war [the Russo-Turkish War of 1876–78] must go on uninterruptedly till the Turkish government is entirely subverted."[3] Yet Smith continued to predict in his editorials that Turkey would collapse ere long and expressed the view that the Second Coming was just around the corner.[4] It was these comments that led White to publicly confront Smith two days after an editorial by him on the Eastern Question appeared in the September 26, 1878, issue of the *Review.*

Milton C. Wilcox and William C. White, both of whom attended the camp meeting and witnessed the confrontation, left records of what they observed. Smith stated during the camp meeting that the Russo-Turkish War of 1876–78 (then in progress) would see the demise of the Ottoman Empire and the close of probation. This would be followed soon after by the Second Coming.[5]

According to Wilcox, White followed Smith's presentation

with a "seventy-minute" rebuttal. White's refutation was published in the *Review* of October 3, 1878. Here is the nub of his argument:

> If the feet and ten toes of the metallic image [of Dan. 2] are Roman, if the beast with ten horns that was given to the burning flames of the great day be the Roman beast, if the little horn which stood up against the Prince of princes be Rome, and if the same field and distance are covered by these four prophetic chains, then the last power of the eleventh chapter [of Dan.], which is "to come to his end and none shall help him," is Rome. But if this be Turkey, as some teach, then the toes of the image of the second chapter are Turkish, the beast with ten horns of the seventh chapter represents Turkey, and it was Turkey that stood up against the Prince of princes in the eighth chapter of Daniel.

White's rebuttal was "To be continued." It never was. Why? W. C. White tells us why. He says that his mother, Ellen White, was shown in vision that her husband erred in confronting Smith publicly. The unity of the church was more important than a private interpretation of a controversial prophecy. As a believer in his wife's divine inspiration, James accepted her rebuke without a murmur and dropped the subject without so much as offering a reason or explanation.[6]

Many years after her husband's death, Ellen White wrote:

> My husband had some ideas on some points differing from the views taken by his brethren. I was shown that however true his views were, God did not call for him to put them in front before his brethren and create differences of ideas. While he might hold these views subordinate him-

self, once [they were] made public, minds would seize [upon them], and just because others believe differently would make these differences the whole burden of the message, and get up contention and variance.[7]

Arthur L. White, Ellen White's grandson, states that one of the points of disagreement between James White and his brethren was their interpretation of the last power of Daniel 11. In his biography of his grandmother, Arthur says that James White

and Uriah Smith held conflicting views on the prophecy of the "king of the North" pictured in Daniel 11 . . . [and that James] felt that Smith's approach, indicating that the world was on the verge of Armageddon, would threaten the strong financial support needed for the rapidly expanding work of the church.

Ellen White's message to her husband was a reproof for taking a course that would lead the people to observe differences of opinion among leaders and to lower their confidence in them.[8]

Did Ellen White Endorse Smith's View?

Because Ellen White reproved her husband for publicly confronting Smith, some have concluded that she agreed with Smith's interpretation and rejected that of her husband. But this is not necessarily the conclusion to be drawn. Ellen White was ever loath to take sides on side issues—and especially when her husband was involved. So far as she was concerned, the unity of the church was more important than the identification of the king of the north. That was true then, and it is true today.

1. *RH,* Feb. 25, 1873.

2. *ST,* Nov. 15, 1877.

3. *RH,* Jan. 24, 1878.

4. See also *RH,* Feb. 7, 1878; Ibid., May 9, 1878; Ibid., June 6, 1878: "Who can fail to see that we have reached the preliminary movements of the great battle of Armageddon?" Ibid., July 11, 1878; Ibid., July 18, 1878, "The attention of the world is beginning to center at Jerusalem, and . . . all events are tending to make the central point in the coming battle of the great day of the Lord"; and Ibid., Sept. 26, 1878.

5. Document File (abbrev. DF) no. 39, Ellen G. White Estate, 12501 Old Columbia Pike, Silver Spring, MD 20904.

6. DF no. 39. Explanation of what happened by W. C. White.

7. *Letter* 37, 1887. (Abbrev. *Lt* 37, 1887). Quoted in Ellen G. White, *Counsels to Writers and Editors* (Nashville, Tenn.: Southern Publishing Association, 1946), pp. 76, 77. (abbrev. *CWE,* pp. 76, 77).

8. Arthur L. White, *Ellen G. White: The Lonely Years* (Hagerstown, Md.: Review and Herald Publishing Association 1984), vol. 3, pp. 96, 97.

CHAPTER
Six

SMITH'S VIEWS BECOME ASCENDANT

When James White died in 1881, no leader of his stature arose to champion his interpretation of Daniel 11. His view that the papacy was the last power of Daniel 11 was virtually abandoned, and Smith's view became the denomination's view for more than seventy years. But there was another factor that increased Smith's influence. In 1882 George King, the first SDA colporteur, urged Smith to combine the 1881 revision of his commentaries on Daniel and the Revelation into a single volume for sale to the public. Already popular among Adventists, these books became the church's standard interpretation of Daniel and Revelation for the next seventy years and beyond.

A Composite Picture of Uriah Smith's Views

In no one place does Smith give a single complete exposition of all the details of his view of Armageddon and the king of the north. However, allowing for an exception or two, his articles and editorials varied little from the position he had taken by 1871.

In outlining the following composite picture of Smith's view it should be remembered that, whereas the principles underlying his view remained more or less constant through the years, there was evolution in the matter of details.

Smith interpreted the Euphrates[1] as well as the "king of the north" of Daniel 11:40-45[2] to be the "Turkish power," "the Ottoman Empire," "Turkey," or pejoratively, "the Turk." He held that, before "Christ's work in the sanctuary closes, and he takes his throne to reign,"[3] "the Turkish power will be compelled . . . to remove its seat of government from Constantinople [now Istanbul] to Jerusalem."[4] This act "would make the 'holy land' . . . the great bone of contention between the Latin, Greek, and Mohammedan religious bodies."[5] After moving to Jerusalem, Turkey would "speedily" come "to its end as a nation."[6] In this national destruction, the nations would "stand aloof."[7] It should be noted that Smith never equated *this* war with Armageddon.

"Shortly after" "the Turk moves to Jerusalem," Smith said, "Christ" finishes "his work as priest."[8] In other words, probation closes and "the plagues begin to fall."[9] Under the sixth vial "everything about . . . [Turkey] which acts as an obstacle to the"[10] "nationalities, powers, and kingdoms lying east of Palestine,"[11] "is entirely consumed."[12]

"The way of the kings of the East" would now be "laid open,"[13] and they would "flow westward."[14] "The spirits of devils [proceeding from] paganism, popery, and a dead and backslidden Protestantism, [would] go forth to gather the nations to the last strife."[15] This war, he said, would "involve all nations."[16]

Interestingly, the ostensible reason for the gathering of the nations in Palestine would be "possession . . . of the sacred sepulchres," on which "the nations have fixed their covetous and jealous eyes."[17] But the real reason would be that the nations "duped" by the "spirits of devils" might engage in "battle against the Lord of hosts."[18] The focal point for this battle would be "the valley of Megiddo."[19] Sometimes, however, Smith said, "the valley of Jehoshaphat, near Jerusalem"[20] would be the storm center.

It has been claimed that Smith never interpreted Armageddon as being a battle of the East against the West. This is incorrect. Although he did not always bring out this aspect of Armageddon, the fact that his interpretation featured the eastern nations moving westward to join the so-called Christian nations and meeting at Megiddo certainly did allow for an East vs. West war. Sometimes, however, Smith did describe Armageddon as a battle in which the hordes of the East attacked the West. For example, he wrote in the *Review* of May 9, 1878:

> So long as the Turkish empire stands, its independence guaranteed by the powers of Europe, so long an effectual barrier remains against the irruption of the modern hordes of the interior of Asia into Western Asia and Eastern Europe. But when Turkey falls, their way will be prepared, the barrier removed; and why may we not expect deluging waves of them to flow westward, as at times in the middle ages?[21]

Enlarging on Uriah Smith's occasional depiction of Armageddon as a battle of the East against the West, T. R. Williamson, a sometime contributor to the church paper, wrote in the *Review* of September 10, 1895:

> I believe the march of the kings of the east is very soon to begin. India will gladly join the westward movement. . . .

The only great obstacle to the march of the eastern swarms is the belt of territory filled with Mohammedans that intervenes between the nations of eastern Asia and the countries of Europe, Turkey, Persia, Afghanistan, and the other countries near to, or bordering upon, the River Euphrates. These will stand or fall together. While they continue in power, especially Turkey, which in influence leads the others, differing as they do in religion from the eastern Asiatics as much as they differ from Europeans, they form a hindering belt, or zone, of strength that keeps Europe and Asia apart. . . .

To defeat the armies and to occupy the land of Turkey, means the division and the rule of her realm by the European nations, the absorption, or drying up, by them of her possessions. That event cannot now be far distant, and that absorption, or drying up of Turkey will prepare the way for the westward roll of the war cloud of Asiatic myriads under their rulers, who are styled in the Revelation, "the kings of the east."

Although Uriah Smith and Williamson and perhaps a few others did allow for an East vs. West Armageddon, this view did not receive any prominence in Adventist thinking until near the end of the Russo-Japanese War of 1904–1905, as we shall show.

The Jones Interlude

In 1897 Alonzo T. Jones, recently returned from a tour of the Holy Land, was elected chief editor of the church paper and Uriah Smith served as his associate. To Smith's Turkish-King-of-the-North/Turkey-Euphrates view Jones soon added a new and very different spin. The principal nations of Europe—the West—which were trying to partition China, plus the United States, which gained possession of the Philippines in 1898, were, according to

Jones, the kings of the east mentioned in Revelation 16:12. Observe how Jones reasoned:

> Russia controls all of North China down to Pikin [Beijing]—all north of the fortieth parallel. Next, to the southward, comes Germany; next to the southward, comes Britain; next, Italy; next, France. *And now,* with Britain and Germany, as well as by her own new possession of the Philippines, there comes in also *the United States* as one of the "kings of the East," Thus the kings of the East are NOW the very ones which have always been the kings of the West; yea, the powers of the extreme West have now become the powers of the extreme East. . . . The power in the Euphrates country [Turkey] ceases to exist [under the sixth plague] "that the way of the kings of the East might be prepared." And, when they come, how many come?—"The kings of the earth and of the whole world." Ah, the kings of the East are the kings of the West; and the kings of the West are the kings of the East! And the same identical kings are the kings of the whole world.[22]

This curious bit of logic never gained much popularity among Adventists, and the view was abandoned as soon as Smith replaced Jones as chief editor of the church paper in 1901. During the next two years until his death, Smith continued to set forth from time to time in his editorials his views of Armageddon and the king of the north.[23] Although he died in 1903, his views lived on for more than fifty years.

Roderick S. Owen's Extension of Smith's View

Late in 1902, Roderick S. Owen, one of the editors of *Signs,* advanced a unique view of the battle of Armageddon. Because his interpretation tried to bring together a variety of views under the umbrella of Uriah Smith's eschatological view, it merits being quoted at length because it goes well beyond what Smith taught. After quoting Zechariah 14:1-3, Owen wrote:

> In these verses we learn that all nations are to be gathered against Jerusalem to battle, and that the city will be taken, after which the Lord will go forth against the nations. This divides the battle into two parts in which three powers are involved. (1) Some power which is in possession of the city, and which suffers a defeat; (2) the nations which attack the city and are victorious, dividing the spoil in the city; (3) the Lord goes against the victorious nations. . . .

Basing his interpretation on Zechariah 14, Owen divided the battle into two parts, in which three powers are involved.

> In Rev. 16:14-16 the spirits of devils, under the sixth plague, go forth to the kings of the earth and the whole world to gather them to the battle of the great day of God Almighty. And they are gathered into a place called Armageddon. . . . Both Joel and Zechariah locate the battle at Jerusalem. . . .
>
> [T]he drying up of the water as a symbol would indicate the overthrowing of . . . [the Turkish] power, and the cutting off of its people. . . .

As for Revelation 16, the gathering of the nations at Jerusalem takes place under the sixth plague, and the drying up of the Euphrates represents the cutting off of the Turkish power and people.

> [T]he prophet Daniel (ch. 11:44, 45) in describing the

career of this power under the title of the king of the north, says: "But tidings out of the east and out of the north shall trouble him: therefore he shall go forth with great fury to destroy, and utterly to make away many. And he shall plant the tabernacles of his palace between the seas in the glorious holy mountain; yet he shall come to his end, and none shall help him."

This text, then, teaches that the Turk will transfer his capital to Jerusalem, and . . . shall come to his end, for none shall help him. . . .

Owen interpreted the Last Power of Daniel 11 to be the Turk, who would move his capital to Jerusalem, where he would come to his end.

The Christian world looks upon the Mohammedan [Turkish] power as antichrist, and this is true in so far as he is opposed to Christianity. But is he the antichrist which is to appear in the world just before Christ comes? . . .

[T]he manifestation of the mystery of iniquity could only be complete with the personal appearing of Satan among men. . . .

When Satan has led the nations to believe that he is Christ, the question will arise, Where is antichrist? Satan will then point to the Mohammedan power, and contend that it constitutes antichrist. And behold, it is in possession of Jerusalem, the holy city. . . . Under the deception that Satan is Christ, and that Jerusalem rightly belongs to him, the nations . . . will unite in sending their armies against the Turk, and he shall come to his end and none shall help him. Thus will the waters of the great River Euphrates be dried up; thus will the way of the kings of the East be prepared, that they may have a part in the last and more important phase of this battle of Armageddon. And Zech. 14:1, 2 will be fulfilled.

To summarize, according to Owen, although Christians might look on Islam led by Turkey as the antichrist, the real antichrist is Satan. When Satan appears as Christ, the question will be: Where is antichrist? and Satan will point the nations of Christendom to Islamic Turkey as antichrist and urge them to send their armies to regain Jerusalem, their rightful possession. In the ensuing war the Turk comes to his end unaided and in this manner the waters of the symbolic Euphrates are dried up. This prepares the way for the kings of the east to act their part in the battle of Armageddon.

> Jerusalem will then be in the hands of the nations, but God has said . . . that all who burden themselves with it shall be cut to pieces, tho all the people of the earth be gathered against it. Zech. 12:2, 3. . . .
> [W]hen the nations have taken the city, the question of which one of them shall possess it, and who shall stand at the head, is still unsettled. . . . [H]aving no common foe, they turn upon each other, and the armies are cut to pieces. . . .
> Other scriptures describe this battle, and show that the results are not confined to Jerusalem. . . . [W]hile the destruction begins at Jerusalem, it is carried to the ends of the earth. The evil which goes forth from nation to nation is the spirits of devils spoken of in Rev. 16:14.

After Jerusalem is captured the nations will quarrel over possession of the city and turn upon each other, and their armies are cut to pieces. But the battle will not be confined to Jerusalem. It will involve the whole earth.

At the close of the battle two of the classes participating in it will be cut off, to wit, the Turk and the nations. The third part or portion of God's people are brought through, and refined, thus fulfilling Zech. 13:8, 9.[24]

This eschatological expansion of Uriah Smith's view never gained many adherents. Owen, in fact, was taken to task for his efforts by Milton C. Wilcox, the chief editor of *Signs,* and one of the few holdouts for the Papacy-the-King-of-the-North view. In his critique of Owen's article, which appeared in the same issue of *Signs,* Wilcox observed:

The theory herein set forth which makes the Turkish power "the king of the north" is the view generally held by prophetic expositors, but to the minds of the editor of this paper, it is open to serious question. . . . To the writer of these articles the above suggestions were made, and it was further suggested that the reference to the "king of the north," the Turkish power, be omitted from the article; but the writer thought the matter in question was essential to the argument. We raise this question, and leave it with the reader, whether the prophecy is not as truly met with the Papacy as the king of the north, the possession of Jerusalem, against which the kings of the earth unite.

The East Against the West View

As previously pointed out, although Uriah Smith's view of Armageddon certainly allowed for an East vs. West battle, and occasionally Smith and others portrayed Armageddon as a battle of the East against the West, this view did not gain many adherents until after the Russo-Japanese War of 1904–05. What happened is that toward the end of this conflict the East vs. West view of Armageddon was *emphasized*. Also, it is not true, as some have claimed, that W. A. Spicer introduced the East vs. West view of Armageddon into Adventist thinking. It is true, however, that *after* World War I he was one of the chief promoters of this view.

George I. Butler First to Emphasize Armageddon as East vs. West

George I. Butler, former General Conference president, appears to have been the first to resurrect and emphasize the idea that Armageddon would be a war of the East, led by Japan, against the "Christian civilization" of the West. Writing in 1905 near the end of the Russo-Japanese War, he suggested:

> It is not impossible that[,] when under the leadership of . . . [the Japanese] now holding back, yea, defeating, the mighty armies of Russia, a great and mighty movement may be inaugurated which would show a wonderful amount of life in the "kings of the East." That term describes Japan and China better than any other that could be found. . . .
>
> Meantime "the yellow peril" is worth studying, and will bear watching. May not the preparation of the forces to participate in the great final battle of Armageddon now be going forward? The vast heathen world will be prominent in it. The millions upon millions of Mohammedans will mingle in the fray. The millions of soldiers of the great "Christian civilization" will act a prominent part. The carnage will exceed anything this world has ever seen. It will be the last great struggle before Christ appears.[25]

The expression "the yellow peril" was a term coined by Kaiser Wilhelm II in 1895 to frighten Europe by raising the specter of the hordes of the East attacking the West.

From 1905 until the beginning of World War I Butler's view gained some adherents, but, as World War I broke on the horizon of history, it didn't fit—the nations were not divided East vs. West but rather Allies vs. Central Powers. The Allies, which consisted largely, but not entirely, of western nations, included China and Japan—eastern nations. Similarly, the Central Powers, the German and Austro-Hungarian Empires, were western nations, yet included Turkey—a largely eastern nation—as their ally. As a consequence, this view went into eclipse until after the war, when it experienced a rebirth.

The Italo-Turkish War of 1911–12

For decades the waning Ottoman Empire had been losing province after province in North Africa. In 1911 France and Germany came close to going to war over the French occupation of Morocco. Soon after, Italy demanded that Turkey cede Cyrenaica and issued an ultimatum to the Sultan. The result was the Italo-Turkish War of 1911–12. Adventists saw the involvement of Turkey in these disputes, and especially the shrinking of its empire, as an apocalyptic sign that the end of the Ottoman Empire was at hand, Armageddon would follow, after which Christ would come.

Beginning in January 1912, Percy T. Magan, a prominent SDA physician and administrator, began publishing a series of articles on the Eastern Question in the monthly edition of the *Watchman*. In these articles he stressed Russia's desire for a warm-water seaport, her designs on the Bosporus and the Dardanelles, and her peoples' rallying cry, "Rasplata"—pay back! These articles appeared every month throughout that year. Said he in his concluding article:

The events of the fall of 1908 marked the turning of the tide and the dawning of a new and a darker day—a day in which the powers plan to dismember that which they once sought to preserve [Turkey]; a day which will surely end, not only in the dismemberment of the Ottoman Empire, and the driving of the Turk out of Europe, but also in the long looked for "last war," the "final catastrophe," in which all those great nations . . . will perish in the ruin and the wreck when ARMAMENTS END AT ARMAGEDDON.[26]

The series was quite sensational.

Beginning with the Nov. 14, 1912, issue of the *Review,* Arthur G. Daniells, president of the General Conference, began a series of articles outlining the accepted Adventist view of eschatology—the Turk would lose all of his possessions in Africa and Europe, after which he would set up his capital in Jerusalem, where he would come to his end with none to help him—then, Armageddon!

The end of the Italo-Turkish War late in 1912 brought a lull in international tensions, but not for long.

World War I Not Armageddon

Early in the summer of 1914 the "Balkan Powder Keg," as that region of the world was called, exploded after the assassination of Archduke Ferdinand in Sarajevo, capital of Bosnia-Herzegovina. The death of the archduke was a serious breach of the peace. During a month of frenzied diplomatic activity, valiant efforts were made to avert war, and for a time it looked as if these might succeed. But, when Austria declared war on Serbia, the die was cast. By August 4, 1914, the major combatants had declared war. After this, there was no turning back.

Despite the fact that some non-Adventist Christians and even secular journalists called the war Armageddon, Adventists wisely did not—*at first.*[27] There were many reasons for this: The Turk had not been driven from Europe and set up his capital in Jerusalem, hence, probation had not closed. After probation closes the plagues fall, and the plagues had not begun to fall. Further, the nations did not gather for Armageddon until the sixth plague, and not even the first plague had fallen. Last but not least, Armageddon would be fought, not in Europe, but in Palestine—Megiddo to be exact. So, we reasoned, this war could not possibly be Armageddon—even if it was the greatest war ever.

However, when Turkey entered the war on the side of the Central Powers late in 1914, our views began to change. Some Adventists began to predict that, as a *result* of the war, Turkey would be driven from Europe and the pieces of the puzzle of the prophecies of Daniel 11 and Revelation 16 would somehow fall into place. As the war progressed, Adventist predictions became more definite. Here is a sampling of some of them:

The decision has been made that the Turk must leave Europe. The decree has gone forth.[28]

Every indication that we have in history and in reports of foreign policies of nations of the East, establishes the fact that the Turk must leave Europe.[29]

The Turk cannot possibly remain in Constantinople. God's word says that he will be forced to move out eventually—and that "eventually" is not far distant.[30]

In fairness to these prognosticators, it should be pointed out that most of them hedged their bets, but not all. One prominent man, for instance, declared:

The great deciding blow will be to drive her [Turkey] from Constantinople, the capital of her empire. The war now raging is designed to accomplish this; and when it is brought about, there will be but one more great act in the drama,— the final and utter destruction of the Ottoman Empire.[31]

At the time this prediction was made, there seemed to be every reason to expect it to be fulfilled, and soon.

The Dardanelles Expedition

In 1915, during the early days of the Dardanelles Expedition, British and French naval squadrons were on the verge of forcing passage through the straits to aid their ally, Russia—and almost succeeded. In fact, it was learned after the war, that the forts protecting the straits had fewer than twenty armor-piercing shells and were preparing to surrender when the British and French withdrew their warships.

Adding to Adventist excitement and anticipation was the fact that it became known that Turkish Sultan Muhammad VI had contingency plans for evacuating Constantinople and moving his capital to Brusa in Asiatic Turkey. There seemed to be every prospect that the predictions Adventist evangelists had been making for years were going to be fulfilled very soon.

In his book, *Adventist Evangelism in the Twentieth Century,*[32] Howard B. Weeks describes how our North American publishing houses cooperated in our evangelistic thrust:

The Southern Publishing Association announced a new tract entitled "Is it Armageddon?" The Pacific Press Publishing Association published the tract "Have We Come to Armageddon?" The Review and Herald Publishing Association produced an extra edition of the church paper entitled "Eastern Question Extra," having just previously published a "War" extra, of which an impressive 1.5 million copies were distributed.

Weeks continues:

There was an inspired conviction that, after many years of ridicule as forecasters of world catastrophe in the face of the world betterment views of other churches, actual events had at last proved the Adventists right and the others wrong. Adventists hastened to press their advantage by calling on unhappy members of other churches to join them in their great movement. The denomination was caught up in a new spirit of confidence, unity, and commitment.[33]

A few pages further on, Weeks says:

A 1917 survey revealed that during the year major evangelistic campaigns had been conducted in more than half of America's seventy-one cities of 100,000 population or more; and plans were afoot to cover the rest during the next year or so. The denomination thrilled to the prospect of continuing advance.[34]

Seeing what they perceived to be "the handwriting on the wall," backsliders were reclaimed, fence-sitters made decisions for Christ, and converts from other churches joined the ranks of the Adventists by the thousands. Noting the success of our evangelistic efforts, the *Christian Advocate* of Nov. 4, 1915, couldn't resist taking a jab at our evangelists as it cast a jaundiced eye at the success of our proselytizers. Said the *Advocate:*

There are 125,844 Seventh-day Adventists, and the net gain last year was ten percent, an accelerated increase which is no doubt partly attributable to the partial success of those evangelists who are reading the morning paper with one eye on the book of Daniel.[35]

This rueful dig, of course, alluded to the habit of our preachers finding in the daily newspapers confirmation of our predictions concerning the king of the north of Daniel 11.

Statistics show that during the years from 1910 through 1917 the membership of the Seventh-day Adventist Church increased 43 percent. However, things did not continue to go so well in the last year of the war, when it became clear that the war was winding down and Armageddon was not going to ensue—at least not right away. Thus, in the late teens and the decade of the 20s, there was an alarming decrease in total membership in the church. But more on this later.

"Allenby of Armageddon"

When the British and French naval forces withdrew from the Dardanelles, after suffering moderate losses from Turkish forts guarding the straits, a lull in the Gallipoli Campaign set in, and never after were the Allies able to regain the initiative. One of the consequences of the Gallipoli fiasco was that Winston Churchill, First Lord of the Admiralty, lost his position in the British cabinet.

After nearly a year of desultory fighting, the British, Anzac,[36] and French colonial troops on the Gallipoli Peninsula withdrew under cover of darkness. Transported to Egypt, they were placed under the able leadership of General Edmund Allenby, later nicknamed "Allenby of Armageddon."

Upon assuming command of these forces, Allenby led his army into Palestine, winning victory after victory as he went. After capturing Beersheba, he turned west and drove the Turks out of Gaza—places familiar to Adventist Bible students. Then, bypassing Jerusalem, he punched his way northward, occupying Jaffa (now Tel-Aviv) on November 16. He then wheeled toward the southeast and headed toward the Holy City—Jerusalem!

According to Adventists living at the time, the hopes and fears of our people reached a fevered pitch during these momentous days. We were sure that in the very near future the Turk would move "the tabernacles of his palace" to Jerusalem and "come to his [ignominious] end." This event would signal the close of probation, Armageddon would follow, and Christ would come—perhaps within a year; two at most.

Allenby's forces approached Jerusalem in early December 1917 and on the 9th entered the Holy City *without firing a shot!* The Turkish troops had hastily withdrawn to the north and it soon became evident the Turk was not going to set up the tabernacles of his palace in the glorious holy mountain any time soon. In the light of these developments, the hopes and fears of our people turned to despair or relief as the case might be.

After taking Jerusalem, Allenby pursued the Turks northward and fought a battle at Megiddo, where he earned the sobriquet—"Allenby of Armageddon." Measured by any standard, the action was anticlimactic and minor, nevertheless the name stuck.

Perhaps Francis McLellan Wilcox, chief editor of the church paper, best expressed the disappointment of many Adventists when Jerusalem fell into British hands, when he wrote:

These are days in which we do well not to hazard too much speculation regarding the trend of events in the world. This war has afforded a long and continued series of surprises. The forecasts of the best-informed men have come to naught. It is better for us to await patiently the progress of human history in the unfolding of God's plan, than to run ahead of his providence and make statements which time may demonstrate to have been only idle speculation.[37]

These words of caution were a little late in coming. But in spite of their tardiness, some Adventists continued to insist that somehow, they didn't know just how, the Turk would yet set up the tabernacles of his palace in the "Holy City." Wrote one confident writer:

Whether the Allies or the Central Powers win this war, the Turk must ultimately leave his present capital, Constantinople. Where will he go? Where can he go and establish another capital? He can go to his Asiatic territory, and nowhere else. And once there, the most likely city, and the most cherished city, for his capital is Jerusalem. This is the "glorious holy mountain" of Scripture. . . . The prophecy will be fulfilled. . . .

The fact that the British forces have recently taken Jerusalem from the Turks may not in the end present any serious obstacle to the fulfillment of this interpretation of the prophecy.[38]

The Greco-Turkish War of 1919–1922

On October 30, 1918, Turkey signed the Mudros Armistice. Soon after, the Allies occupied Istanbul, and Mohammed VI placed himself under the protection of Britain and France. The Allied Powers then encouraged Greece to dismember the "sick man of the East."

The following May (1919) a Greek army landed at Smyrna under the protection of British, French, and American naval guns and proceeded to carve up Turkey. It looked as if after all "the sick man of the East" at long last was coming to his ignoble end with none to help him, just as we had long predicted.

And then, "the best laid schemes o' mice and men" began to go "agley."[39] First, the United States, disgusted with the bickerings of the European powers, backed out of the League of Nations and withdrew its naval forces from Smyrna. But more important, Mustafa Kemal Pasha, leading a nationalist uprising against the Sultan and the Allies, fought a three-week battle (July-August, 1921) against the Greeks and drove the latter into the Aegean. But more humiliating, in 1922 Turkey dictated the terms of the Treaty of Lausanne to the disconcerted Allies. It was a bitter pill—not only for the greatest powers in Europe, but also for our people. But let us go back a bit.

Apostasies Result From the Failed Predictions

In 1918, with the defeat of the Central Powers a virtual certainty, the prospects of an early Armageddon, or the demise of the Turk, faded in the minds of most of those who had been scared into joining the church as a result of our predictions. As a consequence, baptisms plummeted and apostasies skyrocketed. In a letter to Irwin H. Evans, vice president of the North American Division, G. C. President A. G. Daniells wrote in consternation:

> I count it a very serious thing to have so many thousands of people going away from our ranks. . . . It does seem to me that we should somehow find the real cause of this very heavy drift away from us, and set ourselves resolutely to stop it.[40]

In spite of valiant efforts by the denomination's leaders to stanch the flow of the church's lifeblood, baptisms were few and apostasies many in the years that followed.

65

The 1919 Bible Conference

A few months after World War I came to an end, and while the Allies and the Greeks still had the upper hand in Turkey, the General Conference convened a closed Bible conference in Takoma Park, Maryland. These meetings were restricted to senior college Bible teachers, publishing leaders, church administrators, and a few others. There can be little question but that the principal reason for calling this meeting was the embarrassment we had brought on ourselves by the failure of our predictions concerning Turkey. The agenda as well as the transcript of the conference supports this conclusion.

While various topics were discussed at this convocation, such as the daily, the covenants, and the 1260 years of Daniel 7, it is clear that the main purpose for calling the conference was to study whether or not Turkey was indeed the last power of Daniel 11:40-45. Discussions on this topic went under the title of "The Eastern Question."

Perhaps Herbert Camden Lacey, at the time a Bible teacher at Washington Missionary College (now Columbia Union College), put it best when he said, "Daniel 11 is the biggest thing among us at the present time."[41] His statement is supported by the fact that the preponderance of lectures presented had to do with the Eastern Question, not the daily, as some have claimed.

The chief proponents of the Papacy-King-of-the-North view were, not surprisingly, Milton C. Wilcox and Lacey. The chief champions of the Turkey-King-of-the-North view were C. M. Sorensen and A. O. Tait. A handwritten notation on page 275 of the White Estate copy of the "Transcript" states that "the first part of his [Sorensen's] presentation [on the Eastern Question] was not reported, by direction of the Chairman, A. G. Daniells." The reason for this omission is a tantalizing question.

From the comments appearing in the transcript, it is clear

that most of the attendees inclined to the Papacy-King-of-the-North view. However, since the Greeks still had the upper hand in their war with Turkey, and the Turk might yet be launched on his "odyssey to Jerusalem," it appears that it was tacitly agreed among those present that we continue to preach the Turkey-King-of-the-North and the Palestinian-Armageddon views.

From the discussion on pages 905-913 of the White Estate copy of the "Transcript," it seems clear that the primary reason the papers and transcripts of the conference were not published was because of the perplexity they would cause the laity.[42] As a result, Daniells' suggestion "to lock this manuscript up in the vault"[43] was apparently adopted by common consent. There is no evidence that a formal vote was taken to this effect.

Walter T. Knox, General Conference treasurer and chairman of the Bible Conference Committee, concurred with Daniells' opinion when he said, "I believe it would be better not to print it at all,"[44] and that, apparently, ended the matter.

LeRoy E. Froom, editor of the *Watchman,* in a letter to William A. Watson, president of the General Conference (1922–1930), and dated September 18, 1922, said:

Our evangelical periodicals have been reticent about emphasizing Daniel eleven through their columns in the face of divergent views of application, and in view of the agreement at the gathering of Bible and history teachers some three years ago. It was there understood, I believe, that we were to refrain from *publication* of views antagonistic to the position of Turkey as king of the North pending further study, further developments, and in the anticipation of unanimity of belief and teaching.[45]

Froom had been correctly informed. Because of the consensus at the close of the Bible Conference, the transcript disappeared from sight until 1974, when this author asked Donald F. Yost, General Conference director of Archives and Statistics, if there were any records of the 1919 Bible Conference and Yost discovered the transcript and brought it to light.

As a result of the decision taken at the Bible Conference, our evangelists, Bible teachers, and ministers continued to teach for years to come that Turkey was the last power of Daniel 11 and that Armageddon would be a great war in the Middle East.

Interpretations in Disarray

As previously mentioned, against all probability or expectation, the Turks turned tables on the Allies in the Greco-Turkish War of 1919–1922. True, the Ottoman Empire came to an end, but out of its ashes arose, phoenixlike, a vigorous Turkish Republic. This made a shambles of our interpretations of Daniel 11. Leon A. Smith, son of Uriah Smith, probably expressed best the chagrin our people felt, when he lamented:

> Only yesterday it appeared that the final hour for the "sick man of the East" had arrived. The threat made by the Allied powers when Turkey entered the World War, that such action on her part would result in her dismemberment at the close of the conflict, seemed about to be realized. But today a Near East peace treaty [Lausanne] is concluded, by the terms of which Turkey has imposed her will upon the greatest powers of Europe. . . .
>
> The Ottoman power . . . continues to defy the calculations of statesmen and the precedents of history. The "king of the north" still remains a sign to the world, and will continue thus until, after having planted "the tabernacles of his

palace between the seas in the glorious holy mountain," "he shall come to his end, and none shall help him."[46]

That somehow Turkey was still the king of the north continued to be not only Leon Smith's position but the position of most Adventists. After all, our people reasoned, Turkey still retained the Caliphate—the religious leadership of the Islamic world. Referring to this fact Frank A. Coffin editorialized in the *Present Truth* (1917–1955) of June 1, 1925:

> It is true that as a result of the war of 1914-1918 Turkey lost all her territory on the lower Euphrates and in Palestine, but the inhabitants of the region are intensely Mohammedan, and must be reckoned with in any permanent settlement that can be made. . . . Some sudden uprising, not in Turkey only, but of the whole Mohammedan world, might change many of the results of the Great War as affecting Turkey, and at least temporarily restore to that power the possession of the Euphrates valley and Palestine.

But it was not to be. On March 3, 1923, the Turkish parliament abolished the Caliphate. Our interpretation of Daniel 11:45 was in embarrassing disarray. Heretofore the church paper had regularly carried articles on the Eastern Question in its pages, but during 1924 the *Review* carried not a single article on Armageddon or the king of the north.

Some, however, continued to insist that, so long as Turkey retained control of the headwaters of the Euphrates, it was the nation symbolized by that river.

Prophetic Emphasis Shifts to Russia and Japan

As Communism rose to prominence in Russia during the

1920s and 1930s, our emphasis on Armageddon reverted to the East vs. West military conflict at Megiddo introduced by G. I. Butler in 1905. Edwin R. Thiele, the noted biblical chronologist, was the first to resurrect this view. This is what he wrote in the *Signs:*

> The efforts being put forth to weld the entire Orient into one vast revolutionary block that may bid successful defiance to the Western world, seem to have the prospect of success. Russia has already thrown down the gauntlet, and apparently it is in no mood to desist from the course she marked out for herself. . . . It seems to be only a question of time till it will extend itself still farther to enclose both India and China, and the circle of "Red" will close in to include all. That is the day for which Russia is waiting. Then woe to the Western world![47]

But Russia was not the only threat to world peace. Japan, a rising naval power during the 1920s, was making its presence felt in the international community. As a result, some believed that Japan, rather than Russia, would lead the "kings of the East" to Armageddon. Still others believed it might be China, the sleeping giant of the Orient. After all, hadn't Napoleon Bonaparte more than a century before warned Europe of what would happen when the "sleeping giant" of the East wakes up?

---

1. *RH,* June 18, 1857; Ibid., Dec. 2, 1862.
2. *RH,* Oct. 11, 1898; cf. Ibid., Aug. 24, 1897.
3. *RH,* Dec. 20, 1892.
4. *RH,* May 26, 1901.
5. *RH,* June 9, 1891; cf. Ibid., June 18, 1897; Ibid., Dec. 2, 1862.
6. *RH,* Mar. 29, 1887.

7. *ST,* May 3, 1877.

8. *RH,* Mar. 30, 1897; cf. Ibid., Dec. 20, 1892.

9. *RH,* Dec. 20, 1892.

10. *RH,* Dec. 20, 1892.

11. *RH,* Dec. 2, 1862.

12. *RH,* Dec. 20, 1892; cf. Ibid., Jan 24, 1878; Ibid., Mar. 26, 1901.

13. *RH,* Nov. 9, 1876.

14. *RH,* May 9, 1878.

15. *RH,* Nov. 9, 1876.

16. *RH,* Nov. 18, 1875.

17. *RH,* Dec. 2, 1862.

18. *RH,* June 25, 1857.

19. *RH,* Dec. 2, 1862.

20. *RH,* Apr. 7, 1885.

21. Cf. *RH,* June 21, 1864; Ibid., April 11, 1865; Ibid., Feb. 13, 1866; Ibid., June 6, 1866; Ibid., Jan. 15, 1867.

22. Alonzo Trevier Jones, *The Marshalling of the Nations* (Battle Creek, Mich.: Review and Herald Publishing Association, 1900), pp. 36, 37. Emphasis his.

23. For example: *RH,* May 26, 1901; Ibid., Jan. 28, 1902; Ibid., Feb. 11, 1902; Ibid., Feb. 10, 1903; and Ibid., Feb. 17, 1903.

24. *ST,* Dec. 24, 1902.

25. *The Southern Watchman,* Jan. 3, 1905. (Abbrev. *SW;* name varied, such as *The Watchman,* but all abbrev. *SW.*)

26. *SW,* Dec., 1912, p. 732.

27. See, for example, F. M. Wilcox editorials in *RH,* Aug. 13, 1914; *RH War Extra,* Aug. 24, 1914; *RH,* Aug. 29, 1914; Ibid., Sept. 3, 1914; article by G. I. Butler in Ibid., Sept. 15, 1914; article by C. M. Snow in Ibid., Sept. 17, 1914; Sept. 14, 1914; Milton C. Wilcox editorial in *ST,* Aug. 25, 1914.

28. Arthur G. Daniells in *ST,* April 11, 1916.

29. I. H. Evans in *SW,* Sept. 1916.

30. F. I. Richardson in *ST,* Oct. 23, 1917.

31. A. G. Daniells in *Present Truth* (1917–1955), Nov. 15, 1917. (abbrev. *PT* (1917–1955).)

32. Howard B. Weeks, *Adventist Evangelism in the Twentieth Century* (Hagerstown, Md.: Review and Herald Publishing Association, 1969), p. 80.

33. Ibid., p. 81.

34. Ibid., p. 97.

35. Quoted in Ibid., p. 97.

36. Anzac, an acronym for Australian and New Zealand Army Corps.

37. *RH,* Dec. 20, 1917.

38. Arthur G. Daniells, *A World in Perplexity* (Washington, D.C.: Review and Herald Publishing Association, 1918), pp. 93-101.

39. Robert Burns, "To a Mouse." *Agley,* Scottish for "askew."

40. *RH,* Jan. 29, 1918.

41. "1919 Bible Conference and Bible Teachers' Council Transcript," p. 1193. (Abbrev.

"Transcript.") (White Estate copy.) On January 26, 1997, I spoke with Lacey's daughter, Mrs. Paul Flemming, who told me that her father was "fired" from his position as a teacher at Washington Missionary College and was sent to China because of his view that the papacy was the king of the north.

42. Ibid., pp. 906-910.

43. Ibid., p. 912.

44. Ibid., p. 913.

45. The original of this letter is in the SDA Office of Archives and Statistics, General Conference of Seventh-day Adventists, 12501 Old Columbia Pike, Silver Spring, MD 20709. Emphasis his.

In the light of what was happening in the Greco-Turkish War in September 1922, the date of Froom's letter, September 18, may be significant. In the early days of that month the tattered remnants of the Greek army retreated to their base in Smyrna and on the 9th the victorious Turks entered the city. If one can read between the lines, Froom was asking if now it was permissible to identify the king of the north with some power other than Turkey—the papacy, for instance. By now General Conference president A. G. Daniells was out of office.

46. *RH,* Aug. 30, 1923.

47. *ST,* Dec. 11, 1923.

SEVEN

VOICES IN THE WILDERNESS AND WINDS OF CHANGE

Not all Adventists were satisfied with interpretations that shifted with every political wind that blew or fluttered in every sensational newspaper report. Some began to feel that we should study what Ellen White's writings have to say about end-time events in the light of Bible prophecy. Apparently it was with this thought in mind that Carlyle B. Haynes endeavored to merge the accepted view of Armageddon with the description of last-day events given in the Spirit of Prophecy. Said he:

Armageddon is the battle which will decide the controversy between God and the nations, and settle the fate of a rebellious race. . . . When the nations of the earth unite against God, against His people, against His truth, against His law, and "give their power and strength unto the beast," and "make war with the Lamb," then "the Lamb shall overcome them, for He is Lord of lords, and

King of kings." (Rev. 17:13, 14). . . .

   Armageddon is not only the war which will seal the destiny of the human race. It is also the place where this war will be fought. Armageddon means literally the mountain, or hill, of Megiddo. . . . Here the human race is, before long, to fight the battle which will close the history of the world.[1]

   Attempts to harmonize the Spirit of Prophecy description of end-time events with the view of a Palestinian Armageddon were like trying to mix water and oil. Nevertheless such attempts were made from the 1920s to the mid-1970s. Those who tried were voices crying in the wilderness, but at least they were studying what the Spirit of Prophecy says about end-time events.

   One of these wilderness voices was that of Harold E. Snide, a Bible teacher at Union Springs Academy in 1927, who pointed out with remarkable appropriateness that "from being the 'sick man of the East,' Turkey . . . has truly become the 'sick man of prophecy.' "[2]

L. F. Were's View of Armageddon

   In the early 1930s,[3] Louis F. Were, an Australian Adventist evangelist and prolific writer on the subjects of Armageddon and the king of the north, introduced a different interpretation of these prophecies. Because his brethren frowned on his views, he was considered a heretic[4] and was later dismissed from the ministry ostensibly for other reasons. He based his views on hermeneutical principles Adventists had long applied to the prophecies of Daniel and Revelation—but not to the prophecies of the king of the north and Armageddon.

   In his numerous publications, Were frequently pointed out the inconsistencies of his brethren's positions on Armageddon and the king of the north. It is not surprising, therefore, that his forthrightness did not especially endear him to the "old guard."

Were took the basic position that *"When passing over into the Christian era there is an automatic transition* from literal to spiritual Babylon; from literal to spiritual Jerusalem; from the literal lands of Israel and Babylon to their spiritual antitypes."[5] In other words, Jerusalem now referred to the church, and the king of the north and Armageddon had spiritual connotations.

Perhaps his expositions of Revelation 16:12-16 and Daniel 11:40-45 are set forth most succinctly in his book, *The King of the North at Jerusalem,* in which he says:

> By comparing Rev. 12:12-16 with Rev. 13:5-7 and 12:17 with 17:1, 14, 15 we know that the Revelator describes the coming conflict of the combined forces of Babylon—kings and people—as the flooding of the Euphrates over its banks, threatening to engulf the people of God in ruin. There will be a mighty tide of persecution to turn them from their allegiance to the Lord. Rev. 16:12 refers to the Lord's intervention on behalf of his persecuted people. In their evil work of making "war" on "the remnant" church, the "kings" (mentioned in Rev. 17:13 as giving "their power and strength unto the beast") make *"war with the Lamb,* and the Lamb shall overcome them" (v. 14). That is, *because* they make "war" on His people, "the Lamb" will make "war" against the forces of Babylon (Rev. 19:11-21): this is referred to in Rev. 16:12-16 as *"the battle of* that great day of *God* Almighty . . . Armageddon." . . .
>
> Daniel likens the campaigns of the king of the north to that of the overflowing of a mighty river—the Euphrates—(Dan. 11:40, Am. Trans.): "The king of the north . . . shall sweep through many lands *like an overwhelming flood."* That "flood"

75

will again surge "into the glorious land" (v. 41)—where God's people dwell—and, as in the time of the Assyrians, "the waters of the river [the Euphrates] strong and many . . . shall pass through Judah . . . even to the neck" (Isa. 8:7, 8). . . .

The waters of the Babylonian "flood"—the waters of the great river Euphrates—will flood the land and threaten to engulf "the holy city" (Dan. 11:45; Rev. 11:2). But the Lord Who gave Daniel this prophecy "by the side of the great river". . . when he made the solemn oath that He would end the persecution of His people (Dan. 12:5-7), will dry up the waters of "the great river Euphrates" (Rev. 16:12): the king of the north "shall come to his end, and none shall help him" (Dan. 11:45).[6]

Thus *the ending of the king of the north and the drying up of the waters of the Euphrates refer to the same power:* the doom of the forces of Babylon.[7]

According to Were, the central issue in the gathering of the nations to the battle of Armageddon involves a "fierce conflict between the forces of good and evil over the Law of God"[8] and that this conflict focuses on the Sabbath of the fourth or Sabbath commandment of that law. This is how he put it:

[W]e have shown that Rev. 16:15 is Christ's message to His people *before probation closes,* urging them to stand fast as the forces of Babylon seek to persecute and intimidate them with threats of starvation, imprisonment, violence and with death in the final crisis over the Sabbath.[9]

Were also dealt with the one verse of Revelation 16:12-16, which obviously has spiritual connotations and which believers in a Palestinian Armageddon usually glossed over. The verse,

Revelation 16:15, says: "Behold, I come as a thief, Blessed is he that watcheth and keepeth his garments, lest he walk naked, and they see his shame." This is how Were interpreted it:

> The Lord's servant [Ellen White] applies Rev. 16:15 in connection with "the parable of the wedding garment." . . . "[T]he wedding garment represents the character which all must possess who shall be accounted fit guests for the wedding . . . there is a *preparation* to be made by all who attend. . . .
>
> "Only the covering which Christ Himself has provided, can make us meet to appear in God's presence. This covering, the robe of His own righteousness, Christ will put on every repenting, believing soul. 'I counsel thee,' He says, 'to buy of Me . . . white raiment, that thou mayest be clothed, and that *the shame of thy nakedness do not appear*' " (Rev. 3:18). . . ." (C[hrist's] O[bject] L[essons] 311).
>
> Thus, . . . the Spirit of Prophecy applies Rev. 16:15 in connection with the days of preparation of character while the investigative judgment is still in session and *before probation closes.* . . .
>
> Why, then, is this warning and exhortation mentioned in connection with the sixth plague? When probation closes, the characters of God's people are sealed for eternity. . . . The *watching* and the *keeping of garments* . . . applies now: to the time before the close of probation; to the time when the evil spirits are abroad deceiving the people regarding obedience to the law of God; to the time Satan is uniting the world in rebellion against the claims of God's law.[10]

This explanation brings to light a new and unusual connection between the warning of Revelation 16:15 and the activity of the unclean spirits gathering the kings of the world to Armageddon.

Were believed that enforcement of Sunday laws would fulfill the prophecy of Daniel 11:45.[11] He taught that " 'the glorious holy mountain' refers to the church" of God.[12]

Observe how he interpreted "Edom, and Moab, and the chief of the children of Ammon" of Daniel 11:41:

> "They [God's people] shall lay their hands upon *Edom and Moab; and the children of Ammon* shall *obey* them." [Isa. 11:14.] Notice that these are the very people mentioned in the prophecy concerning the activities of the king of the north—Egypt, Moab, Edom, and the children of Ammon. In Daniel 11:41 we read: "But these shall escape out of his hand [the hand of the king of the north], even *Edom, and Moab, and the chief of the children of Ammon.*" These are the very ones mentioned in the prophecy of Isa. 11 as obeying "the remnant of His [God's] people." That is, through heeding God's last-day message of salvation, they "escape out of his [the king of the north's] hand" and take their stand with the people of God "*inside* Jerusalem," the "holy city [God's remnant church]." . . .
>
> [I]n the loud cry, from among the ranks of God's enemies, souls . . . will yet be saved, to take their stand with God's people. . . . Thus will "these escape out of his hand"—the hand of the Papacy.[13]

Concerning the giving of the third angel's message during the loud cry, Were believed that

> The loud cry will be given with such mighty power that the king of the north will become greatly *troubled* thereby; "*therefore* he shall go forth with *great fury* to destroy, and

utterly to make away many" (Dan. 11:44), and to accomplish his designs he encamps about the spiritual "holy city" [God's remnant church]," but the Lord intervenes to deliver His people.[14]

Were interpreted "Egypt," mentioned in Daniel 11:42, 43, to represent Communism and predicted that Communism would yet come under papal control. Said he:

> Communism is the one great barrier between her [the papacy] and her goal. This barrier she regards as a serious hindrance to the acquisition of world control. This barrier she seeks to remove. The Scriptures declare that she will overcome this tremendous barrier—"the land of Egypt shall not escape": the countries that have adopted "godless" Communism will not escape her [the papacy's] control.[15]

Were predicted that the world would not always be divided the East against the West, but that the West and the papacy would emerge victorious from the Cold War. He came to this conclusion through his study of the Spirit of Prophecy writings. Said he as early as 1951:

> [T]he warning of the third angel against the "worship of the beast and his image" must go to the whole world—including Russia, China, etc. Thus it will be readily seen that a belief in the magnitude of the third angel's Message, a belief that it is a world-wide message, automatically rules out the idea that the world will *remain* divided between "east" and "west" until the sixth plague; and a belief in the world-wide extent and greatness of the third angel's message reveals an understanding of the "great changes" that are destined to take place in present

political conditions, resulting in the exaltation of the Papacy among the nations of the world and the consequent peril and threat of death to God's people *"in all parts of the world"* over the Sabbath—before probation closes.[16]

Were predicted that

The prophetic finger points to Rome and Europe, backed by the mighty power of Protestant America as the *dominating world powers until the very last hours of earthly history.* Rome will "recover her lost supremacy"—*"prophecy foretells a restoration of her power"* (*GC*, 579-581).[17]

Were based his forecast on the writings of Ellen White, and, of course, Revelation 13:3. Notice how he arrived at this conclusion:

"Under one head,—the Papal power,—the people will *unite* to oppose God in the person of His witnesses" (7T 182). This includes Russia, China, etc., in with the rest of the world, for we are explicitly informed in the Spirit of Prophecy: "As America . . . shall unite with the Papacy in forcing the conscience and compelling men to honour the false sabbath, the people *of every country in* [i.e. on] *the globe* will be led to follow her example.[18]

Were further took the position that

Whatever military wars may yet be fought between various nations and if some of the fighting is done in Palestine— even in the Valley of Jehoshaphat or at Megiddo—these wars will have no direct relation to "Armageddon."[19]

Were's eschatological views were very different from those espoused by his brethren—and, it might be added, much closer than theirs to Ellen White's scenario of end-time events and the early Adventist views of Armageddon and the king of the north.

Were was not always as diplomatic as he might have been in presenting his views of Bible prophecy, nor was he always without error in his interpretations. But what is important is that his views concerning the king of the north and Armageddon were largely rejected by his contemporaries, and only in recent years have they received the attention that they deserve. In his defense of his views, *The Trials and Triumph of Truth: My Reply to Misrepresentation,* he predicted:

> [T]he "new theory" of the military Armageddon will yet be abandoned by Spirit-led believers in the closing days of the great struggle.[20]

Time will tell whether or not this prediction comes true.

World War II and Armageddon

Let us go back a few years. Throughout the remainder of the 1930s, Japan was making efforts to subjugate China, and Russian Communism was attempting to subvert the world through Marxism. These events provided ample grist for our evangelistic mills to present to their audiences the view that Armageddon would be a battle of the East against the West. It seemed to matter little whether Japan or the Soviet Union or even China would lead the kings of the East against the West in earth's final battle.

However, as World War II loomed up on the international horizon, the division of the combatants (as in World War I) was not East vs. West but Axis vs. Allies. As a result, the East-West Armageddon view largely, but not entirely, went into eclipse—*until after the war.*

During the war emphasis was placed on an international melee in Palestine, but nothing happened in the war that measured up to our traditional view of Armageddon. So, once again our interpretations concerning this battle were in disarray. Fredrick Lee, an associate editor of the church paper, probably reflected the confusion many of our people felt at this time when he wrote:

The issues that bring on Armageddon will be extremely complex. Through some "ism" or "ideology" whole nations will be whipped into a fanatical state of mind. Nations will not then go to war for gold, or even wheat, but they will go to war because of definite purposes which are akin to religious aspirations. One nation has this "divine mission," another that. All go out to save the world—one, perhaps, to save it for communism; another to save it for fascism; another to save it for Catholicism; another to save it for Christianity; etc.

One's mind becomes confused as one endeavors to figure out an orderly and definite approach to the last great war, such as lining up nations and races upon one side or another.[21]

The pieces of the puzzle simply would not fit the radically different scenarios of Armageddon taught by the advocates of a Palestinian view when compared with the teachings of the Spirit of Prophecy.

Origins of the Bible Research Fellowship

In spite of this disparity, attempts continued to be made to somehow interpret Armageddon as a spiritual battle as well as a military conflict. Such attempts, rather than unifying the church, tended to polarize it. So, by the early 1940s, the winds of change were beginning to blow with increasing force. Raymond Forrest

Cottrell, then a Bible teacher at Pacific Union College Preparatory School (Academy), in a paper tracing the history of the Bible Research Fellowship, summarized the changes that were taking place among Adventists with respect to Armageddon and the last power of Daniel 11. He says:

> In the years leading up to, and including World War II, international events concentrated attention of Seventh-day Adventists on last-day prophecies, particularly the identity of the king of the north of Daniel 11, and the battle of Armageddon in Revelation 16.[22]

At the College Bible Teachers' Council held in Washington, D.C., in the summer of 1940, it was voted to organize a College Bible Teachers' Fellowship. Dues were collected and placed in the hands of "D[enton] E. Rebok at the [Seventh-day Adventist] Seminary, . . . [who] never did anything about the proposed organization."[23]

The "study group at Angwin [, California, continued to meet and] chose the name 'Eschatological Society,' and at its first meeting [held in February 1943] read and discussed . . . [Cottrell's] contextual linguistic study on 'the Kings of the East'."[24] During the winter of 1943–44 some of the teachers at Pacific Union College, led by Dr. Leon L. Caviness, met and discussed papers on various topics, most of which were about Bible prophecies related to end-time events.[25]

When the Bible Teachers' Council met in 1944, the Bible Research Fellowship was organized under the leadership of Caviness, with some forty-seven members, twelve of whom resided at Angwin. The dues in Rebok's safekeeping were turned over to Caviness, and the BRF came into being. Chapters were formed in various denominational colleges. The home chapter remained at PUC but had no official connection with the college.

As time went on the organization grew, and by the time the 1950 Bible Teachers' Council met, it counted a world membership of 204. These included Bible teachers, ministers, denominational workers, and a few non-church workers.[26] "By 1951 the world membership of BRF . . . [had grown to] 250 and included teachers at every SDA college around the world except one; [as well as] . . . [including] seventeen [who were employed] at the G[eneral] C[onference]."[27]

Although small in numbers, the BRF began to exert a wide influence throughout the denomination's colleges, and eventually on Adventist college students. Among the members of the BRF were such well-known men as L. L. Caviness, R. F. Cottrell, T. Housel Jemison, Mead McGuire, Guy F. Wolfkill, H. Camden Lacey, E. R. Thiele, C. S. Longacre, and Edward Heppenstall, to name but a few.

Not all the teachers of the church's colleges took kindly to the views expressed in the papers submitted to the BRF. This was especially true regarding Armageddon and the last power of Daniel 11. It was early during this period that feelings between the "literalists" and the "spiritualists" ran so high that the "battle of push and shove" took place between two college teachers.

The Influence of the Bible Research Fellowship

Although the BRF discussed many and varied topics, many of the papers studied by its members from 1943 to about 1950 dealt with Daniel 11 and Revelation 16.[28]

Some students in Adventist colleges who surreptitiously secured copies of the papers shared by members of the BRF were influenced by what they read. In the spring of 1945 this researcher, then a theology student at PUC, became convinced that Armageddon was a spiritual struggle between the forces of good and evil as the result of reading a pamphlet titled *Armageddon,* by Louis F. Were. The pamphlet, loaned to him by Albert Kephart, an American GI, who had secured a copy in Australia, contained the following clinching statement by Ellen White:

> We need to study the pouring out of the seventh vial. The powers of evil will not yield up the conflict without a struggle. But Providence has a part in the battle of Armageddon. When the earth is lighted with the glory of the angel of Revelation eighteen, the religious elements, good and evil, will awake from slumber, and the armies of the living God will take the field (*Ms.* 175, 189 [now quoted in 7*BC*, 983]).

The students were also swayed by what they heard their Bible teachers discuss in and out of classes. As their concepts concerning Armageddon and the king of the north changed, some church administrators and evangelists became alarmed. They felt that the students were being taught heresy.

Fortunately this was not true of all conferences. And yet, even within "liberal" conferences, there were those who were suspicious of "new view" interns. For example, when the author was taken on as a ministerial intern by the Northern California Conference in the summer of 1949, he was instructed to contact Elder Alden O. Sage, the conference evangelist, under whom he would be laboring. Elder Sage lived at Pacific Union College. When the newly hired intern knocked at the evangelist's door, he was graciously invited in. After initial pleasantries, the evangelist went right to the point. "Young man," he demanded, "what do you believe about Armageddon?" The brash young man replied, "Well, Elder, it makes a good headline, doesn't it?" The young man soon learned that this is not the way to make friends and influence people. Yet, in time, the two became good friends.

Raymond F. Cottrell's Influence on Students

Raymond F. Cottrell, secretary of the BRF (1944–52), exerted considerable influence, not only on his colleagues but on his students as well. As secretary of the BRF, his influence went far beyond PUC.

Cottrell's research into the views of the pioneers of the Seventh-day Adventist Church concerning Armageddon and the king of the north revealed for the first time that the views expressed by Uriah Smith in *D&R* were *not* the original views espoused by the pioneers of the Seventh-day Adventist Church. To the contrary, he brought to light the fact that the view held by James White and the other early church leaders was actually the "old view."

Cottrell also called attention to the fact that although at first Smith held views consistent with those of these early Adventist leaders, it was Smith who shifted positions regarding Armageddon and the king of the north, *not* the pioneers.[29] He also showed that the truly old view was in better agreement with the Spirit of Prophecy than the military view of Armageddon.[30]

In a paper submitted to the BRF in May 1945, titled "Armageddon: A Study in Historical and Prophetic Backgrounds," Cottrell probably set forth the most comprehensive, as well as the most closely reasoned, of all the papers on Armageddon submitted to the BRF. Because of its widespread influence on students, faculty, and others, its most significant portions are here quoted at length:

[N]o battle is fought under the sixth plague; the powers of earth are merely gathered together—led to the very point of executing their plan to annihilate the remnant. The actual "battle of Armageddon" is fought under the seventh plague, when "He on whose vesture is written the name, King of kings, and Lord of lords" will "lead forth the armies of heaven." (6T 406.4) This . . . definitely links Armageddon with Revelation 19:11-21. . . . Satan and his army, sponsored by the three-fold union, are also shown gathered to make war (cf. 12:17; 13:4, 15; 16:13, 14, 16; 19:20). . . .

Another fact of context which should not be overlooked is the time sequence involved, within the sixth plague itself. The cause of the drying up of the river Euphrates is the outpouring of the sixth plague. . . . The Euphrates river is dried up when the angel pours out his vial—not before.

. . . [I]t is to be noted that the plagues are poured out upon those who worship the beast and his image, and who receive his mark in their foreheads or hands (13:14-18; 14:9-11; 15:1, 2). When probation closes there are but two classes of people left on the earth. (TM-465.4; 9T-16.8; etc.) Therefore, the sixth plague, the "drying up" of the Euphrates, must be construed as a part of God's wrath poured out upon that part of earth's inhabitants which is following Babylon . . . .

Historically, the city of Babylon and the river Euphrates are inseparable. The Euphrates was unquestionably the "river of Babylon." Babylon literally "sat" upon many literal waters (Jer. 51:12, 13)—[which] certainly [refers to] the Euphrates river which brought prosperity and protection to the city. . . .

The seven last plagues are definitely stated to be a visitation upon Babylon and her people. . . . Evidently, the waters upon which the sixth angel pours out his plague must . . . refer to the people over whom the papacy holds sway, and who support it.

In regard to the word "Armageddon," . . . there never

actually was a place known by that name, in either the Hebrew or in any other language. Since there never was a place known in Hebrew as Armageddon, it must be that John was speaking symbolically. . . . It may properly be asked, then, why John refers to . . . [Armageddon] as a place? A similar use of the same Greek word here translated "place" (*topon*) is found in Hebrews 12:17, where it is stated that Esau sought a "place" (opportunity, condition, or situation favorable) for repentance, but failed to find it. . . . The kings of the earth, then, are to be gathered together into a situation which might properly be descirbed [i.e., described] to one familiar with Hebrew language and history as Armageddon—the hills of slaughter. . . .

Drying up of the Great River Euphrates

When the principle of historical allusion is applied to the expression "the water thereof was dried up," numerous Old Testament passages are found significant. . . . Exodus 14:16, 21, 22, 29; 15:19. [The drying up of the Red Sea when the Israelites crossed over it on their way out of Egypt] . . . *Joshua 3:17*. [The drying up of the Jordan when Israel crossed over it into the Promised Land] . . . *Isaiah 44:27*. [The drying up of the waters of the Euphrates by Cyrus, when God says of Babylon, "I will dry up thy rivers] . . .

Cyrus is God's agent for the destruction of Babylon and the liberation of His servant Jacob (44:28; 45:4). . . . This is a Messianic prophecy, for Cyrus is called "my shepherd" who will perform all "my pleasure, saying to Jerusalem, thou shalt be built." He is the Lord's annointed [*sic*], to subdue the nations; he is also the "ravenous bird" from the east (45:1; 46:11). . . .

God waits till Satan's subjects desert him (are dried up from him), and then destroys the great river of the great city, together with the city itself. . . . At the opening of the seventh plague the wicked people of earth have surrounded the righteous just at the moment appointed for the execution of the death decree. (EW-285.1; . . .) But when God intervenes they see that they have been deluded, and turn with fury upon their false shepherds the instruments of death which were to be used against the righteous. (GC-656.2; Rev. 16:19; 17:16; Jer. 25:34-38; etc.)

The Kings of the East

. . . [T]he person and work of Cyrus were symbolic of Christ, as when in Isaiah 41:2, 25 God foretold that He would raise up a "righteous man from the east." . . . Notice . . . that in the accomplishment of his appointed task, Cyrus had the promise of God, "I will dry up thy rivers (Isa. 44:27), referring of course to his strategy in taking Babylon. Christ is to use the same strategy in taking modern Babylon. . . .

John repeatedly speaks of Christ as "King of kings" (Rev. 17:14; 19:16; etc.) in connection with events occurring during the "day of the Lord." . . . Therefore . . . He may appropriately be termed, "King" of or from, "the east." It is proper to ask next, then, for the identity of the sub-kings over whom He is to reign as King supreme. . . .

It would seem that the full weight of historical evidence of the Scriptures points to Christ as *the* King of the east, and to the saints as *kings* of the east together with Him. . . .

The Three Unclean Spirits

. . . [T]he three unclean spirits that go forth from its members to the kings of the earth must sponsor Satan's plan, which at that time is to defeat God by subduing His people. These three forces are also pictured in Revelation 13:4, 13-15, under the symbols of the dragon (Spiritualism), the beast (the papacy), and the false prophet or image to the beast (Protestantism). . . .

. . . [S]ince the causes of the battle are religious in nature, it should therefore properly be spoken of as a religious, rather than a political battle. . . .

The Kings of the Earth

The outstanding fact relative to the kings of the earth is they are gathered *together*—not divided each against the other. They are angry at God and united against *Him* (Rev. 16:11, 9; 17:14; 19:11-19). Satan makes war by combining the nations of earth against God's people. . . .

The Battle of the Great Day of God

For a description of the battle itself, it is necessary to go to the seventh plague. First of all, God's voice is heard saying, "It is done!" that is, the wicked of earth have fully demonstrated their opposition toward Him and His people, and He has arrested them in the very act of killing all His chosen ones; therefore He is fully justified in performing His "strange act" of destroying them one and all. . . .

The time appointed in the [death] decree arrives, the crisis when all the powers of earth are arrayed against God's people (GC-634.2). At midnight, just as the wicked rush forward with shouts of triumph, God manifests His power to deliver, and a dense blackness covers the earth (EW-285.1; GC-636.7,1; 1T-354.3; EW-283.6; Isa. 17:12-14). . . . Then, in rapid succession, mighty upheavals of nature take place—as God goes forth to annihilate His enemies. There is a terrible awakening among the wicked as God's voice turns the captivity of His people (GC-562; 654.1; EW-92.2; 266.3; Jer. 25:30, 31). Realizing that they have been deluded, the people begin to accuse one another; but all unite in the bitterest condemnation of their ministers, and these false teachers confess before the world their work of deception (GC-655.9; EW-282.4; GC-656.1). Filled with fury, the multitudes turn upon these false shepherds and upon one another the very weapons with which they intended to slay the righteous. . . .

While the wicked are engaged in this frightful carnage, a small black cloud appears: the sign of the Son of Man (GC-640.8; EW-15.8; 35.3). The clash of arms, the tumult of battle is stilled (GC-642.5; Isa. 9:5; Rev. 6:15-17; Isa. 2:10-21).[31]

It did not take long for many of the teachers and college students to adopt this "new" (actually "old") view, or a modified form thereof. As a consequence, evangelists and church administrators—the "old guard"—felt threatened. Positions they had held for years were being questioned.

Winds of Change

The fall of Japan in 1945, the internal struggle in China between the nationalists and communists in the late '40s, as well as the heating up of the Cold War during succeeding decades, once again saw a shift in the preaching of our evangelists concerning which nation would lead the "kings of the east" to Armageddon. Because of Japan's defeat and China's internal strife, but mainly because the Soviet Union threatened to engulf the world in communism, the mantle of leadership of the eastern nation in the conflict between the East and the West fell on the USSR.

The 1950 Bible Teachers' Council at PUC

Following the 1950 General Conference Session in San Francisco, the Bible Teachers' Council consisting of thirty-two attendees, two from the General Conference, twenty-four from Adventist colleges in North America, and six from Adventist sanitariums in North America, met at PUC from July 23-31. Vernon E. Hendershot, dean of the Seventh-day Adventist Seminary, presided; Louis H. Hartin, head of the PUC theology department, was secretary. The objectives of the council were for "the sharing of information and skills which will make for better teaching, better implementation, of the principles of Christian education within the department of education framework, and the better integration of our departmental programs with the general aims and organization of the individual college."[32] Another important aspect of the council was how to deal with controversial issues.

During the council a "Questionnaire on Divergent Views," hastily prepared by Cottrell, was passed out to those attending. Two of the questions dealt with Daniel 11:40-45 and Armageddon. Of those who responded, not one believed that "The king of the north is Turkey"; thirteen believed that "The king of the north is the papacy"; three believed that "The papacy is the power represented; the kings of the north and south are in addition to the pap[a]cy"; eleven believed that "The king of the north in the last verses is *communism*"— "Russia"; eleven believed that "The king of the south in the last verses is *Mohammedanism*."

As for Armageddon, none believed that it "Is a battle of the nations of east and west"; sixteen believed it "Is essentially a final battle between Christ and Satan, with all the wicked of earth slaying one another in real warfare as Christ appears in the clouds of heaven"; four believed it "Is a 'spiritual battle' without any military significance." None believed that "The waters of the Euphrates represent Turkey"; twelve believed that "The waters of the Euphrates represent people supporting the papacy." None believed that "The kings of the east are earthly powers"; and twelve believed that "The kings of the east are Christ as King of kings and Lord of lords, and those that 'are with him.' Revelation 17:14."

It is clear from these responses that the majority of those present favored the so-called "new views" of the last power of Daniel 11 and Armageddon.[33]

Word concerning Cottrell's questionnaire came to the attention of the president of the General Conference in a roundabout way. It first reached Australia via Louis Were, who claimed that all the Bible teachers at the meeting believed as he did on Armageddon and the king of the north. Administrators in the Australasian Division understood that he had been "an honored guest" at the council. As a result, questions arose concerning Cottrell's part in preparing the questionnaire.

In a paper titled "Louis F. Were at the Bible Teachers' Council and the Questionnaire on Controversial Topics," dated January 11, 1951, Cottrell endeavored to put distance between himself and Were. He denied that the latter was in any way "an 'honored guest' " and explained that the questionnaire had been prepared hurriedly. Nevertheless, he stressed "the unanimous feeling of joy and freedom, that now at long last we all saw eye to eye on some of the problems that had found us divided in years past."[34]

The powers that be did not share the "joy" that Cottrell reported had been experienced by those who attended the council. As a consequence, and also because the "new view" of Armageddon and the king of the north were perceived to be a challenge to the long-held military view, newly elected president of the General Conference William H. Branson sent out word to disband the BRF.[35]

Shortly after this the General Conference called for a Bible Conference to convene in the late summer of 1952. The purpose of these meetings was to restudy matters of concern to the church, including Armageddon.[36] The conference was held in Takoma Park, Maryland, from September 1 to 13. Unlike the 1919 Bible Conference, this conference was open, and the papers presented were published in two books that bore the title *Our Firm Foundation* (Washington, D.C.: Review and Herald Publishing Association, 1953), vols. I, II.

---

1. The monthly *Watchman,* May 1924.

2. Harold E. Snide, *Prophetic Essays* (Union Springs, N.Y.: The Academy Press, 1927), p. 28.

3. In *The Certainty of the Third Angel's Message, Proved by Important Principles of Prophetic Interpretation* (Adelaide: Modern Printing Co., Ltd., 1945), p. 107, Were speaks of his "brochure on 'Futurism and the Antichrist of Scripture.'" This brochure was originally published in Australian *Signs of the Times,* July 1931. In his *What Is Armageddon?* (Adelaide: Modern Printing Co., Ltd., 1942), p. 4, Were says he began his studies on Armageddon "over a decade ago," hence 1931.

4. *The Trials and Triumphs of Truth: My Reply to Misrepresentations* (East Malvern, Victoria, Australia: A. F. Blackman, Print[er], 1956), pp. [1]-[44].

5. Louis F. Were, *The King of the North at Jerusalem* (East Malvern, Victoria, Australia: A. F. Blackman, 1949), p. 75. Italics his.

6. Ibid., pp. 111, 112. Italics his.

7. Ibid., p. 99. Italics his.

8. Louis F. Were, *Before Probation Closes* (East Malvern, Victoria, Australia: A. F. Blackman, Printer, 1951), p. 6.

9. Louis F. Were, *God Speaks and Israel Triumphs* (East Malvern, Victoria, Australia: A. F. Blackman, Printer, 1951), p. 78. Italics his.

10. Louis F. Were, *Before Probation Closes* (East Malvern, Victoria, Australia: A. F.

Blackman, Printer, 1951), pp. 87-90. Italics his.

11.*The King of the North at Jerusalem,* p. 79. Chapter title: "The Enforcement of Sunday Laws Will Fulfil Daniel 11:45."

12. Ibid., p. 68.

13. Ibid., p. 72. Italics his.

14. Ibid., p. 70. Italics his.

15. *Before Probation Closes,* p. 60. Italics his.

16. Ibid., p. 7. Italics his.

17. Ibid., p. 9. Italics his.

18. Ibid., p. 54. Italics his.

On November 16, 1954, on the basis of Ellen White's statements on last-day events, and independently from F. W. Were or any other student of the Spirit of Prophecy writings, this researcher came to the conclusion that the United States would win the cold war. He wrote down his thoughts in a private cipher on a scrap of paper which is still in his possession. Eight years later, on December 25, 1962, he wrote to his brother Charles George Mansell:

> Do you remember the conversation we had on the mall as we walked toward the Washington [M]onument back in the summer of '59? Well, I said that Ellen White says that "the people of every country on the globe["] will be led to follow "the example" of the United States in passing Sunday laws. (See Testimonies [for the Church], Vol. VI, p. 18). I have no more special foresight than anyone else, but on the basis of this statement, which I believe, it is evident that our country has not yet reached the pinnacle of world power she is yet to attain. This being the case, it is evident to me that in some way, I do not profess to know how, the nations which today loom so large in the path of this destiny [e.g., the Soviet Union and China], will some day follow the behest of the United States when she says to them that dwell on the earth "that they should make an image to the beast." (see Revelation 13:14). I believe, and have believed for some time, that all the rocket rattling on the part of Russia is having but one effect—uniting Europe and the United States. When this is accomplished, it would be nothing for Communism to go down suddenly and quite dramatically.

19. Louis F. Were, *Europe and Armageddon! Europe, the World's Storm Center* (East Malvern, Victoria, Australia: A. F. Blackman, Printer, 1949), p. 80.

20. Louis F. Were, *The Trials and Triumph of Truth. My Reply to Misrepresentation,* p. 34.

21. *RH,* Aug. 31, 1939.

22. Raymond F. Cottrell, "The Bible Research Fellowship: A Pioneering Seventh-day Adventist Organization in Retrospect," *Adventist Heritage,* 5:1 (Summer) 1978, p. 40.

23. Letter from Raymond F. Cottrell to Donald E. Mansell, Feb. 13, 1997, p. 2.

24. Ibid.

25. Ibid., p. 1.

26. Raymond F. Cottrell, "The Bible Research Fellowship: Its History and Objectives (A mimeographed paper), pp. 4-8. This paper was prepared for the 1950 Bible Teachers' Council.

Raymond F. Cottrell, "The Bible Research Fellowship" (A mimeographed paper), pp. 2-4.

27. Cottrell letter, Feb. 13, 1997.

28. (Typewritten. No author listed but probably compiled by Raymond F. Cottrell, secretary of the BRF, who gave it to the author), "Papers Presented to the Bible Research Fellowship, 1943-1952," pp. 1-4.

29. Raymond F. Cottrell, "Pioneer Views on Daniel Eleven and Armageddon" (Mimeographed paper sent to members of the Bible Research Fellowship, Revised edition, 1951), pp. 1-29.

30. Ibid.

31. Raymond F. Cottrell, "Armageddon: A Study of Historical and Prophetic Backgrounds," a mimeographed paper presented to the Bible Research Fellowship, Angwin, California, dated in the author's handwriting, "May 1945"), pp. 3-22.

32. V. E. Hendershot, chairman; L. H. Hartin, Secretary, *Report of College Bible Teachers' Council* (Angwin, California: 1950), p. 2.

33. Ibid.

34. Raymond F. Cottrell, "Louis F. Were and the Bible Teachers' Council," a mimeographed paper, Angwin, California, January 11, 1951.

35. The author was present when this was done at the PUC chapter. Paul E. Quimby, a member of the BRF, was of the opinion that the BRF should comply. Elder Cottrell suggested that, like David, the BRF go into hiding for a while. In the end, the majority felt that the BRF should disband, and this was done.

36. On a 3 x 5 slip of yellow paper among the author's source materials is a penciled notation which says: "R. F. Cottrell told me 4/8/71 that it was the furor caused by [Louis F.] Were's claim in Australia that all the Bible teachers in the U.S. held his view of Armageddon, etc., that [prompted] W[illiam] H. Branson to call the 1952 Bible Conference and kill the Bible Research Fellowship." In a telephone conversation with Cottrell on January 18, 1997, Cottrell told this researcher that it was Elder Nathanael C. Wilson, president of the Australasian Division, who wrote Branson about Were being an "honored guest" and that the paper, "Louis F. Were at the Bible Teachers' Council and the Questionnaire on Controversial Topics," was his (Cottrell's) attempt to set matters straight.

EiGHT

THE WAR
OF
ARMAGEDDON

By the time the 1952 Bible Conference convened on the campus of Washington Missionary College (now Columbia Union College), the church was overdue for change concerning our understanding of the prophecies, especially Revelation 16:12-16. Speaking on "The Place of Prophecy in Our Preaching," veteran administrator Albert V. Olson set forth the problem of the king of the north and Armageddon succinctly in these words:

it may not be out of place to sound a note of warning against the danger of yielding to the temptation of indulging in fanciful, private interpretations or personal predictions. Consciously or unconsciously many of us may have erred on this point.

Years ago I overheard one of our ministers, who had frequently written articles for the newspapers of his city [probably Washington, D.C.] on the Turkish question, say to a group of workers, "I will never write another article on this subject for the public press, because every time I tell what the Turk is going to do he makes a fool of me by doing something entirely different." By his erroneous interpretations and his unwarranted predictions, this good brother had created embarrassment both for himself and for the church.[1]

Speculation is futile on who this person might have been.

W. E. Read's War of Armageddon

Walter E. Read, the person chosen to present the topic of Armageddon at the Bible Conference, told this researcher that several months before the conference convened, General Conference President W. H. Branson met him in one of the halls of the church's headquarters, in Washington, D.C., and asked him to prepare a presentation on Armageddon.

Aware of the heat the subject had generated in the past, Read said he accepted the honor with some reluctance. Nevertheless, as a good soldier, he accepted the assignment and began to research the literature. The fruits of his labor appear in the book, *Our Firm Foundation,* vol. 2, pages 239-335, under the title, "The Great Controversy."

A church administrator and scholar of long experience, Read laid the groundwork for his presentation by emphasizing the great controversy theme. He began with Satan's rebellion in heaven and proceeded with its continuation on earth. In his presentation he laid considerable stress on the fact that Armageddon was "a war," not merely a battle. Said he: "The word used to designate this conflict in our Bible is *battle,* whereas the more correct translation of the original word is war."[2] He reiterated this point numerous times throughout his presentation and even added an appendix to emphasize its significance.

Read set forth his findings concerning the war of Armageddon thus:

> The conflict of Armageddon, then, is the "war" (*polemos*) "of that great day of God Almighty." Hence, if we recognize Armageddon as a "war" rather than a "battle," we shall be prepared to recognize a *series* of engagements rather than *one* conflict in this closing struggle.[3]

So Armageddon was *not* a single engagement at the end of the world but a series of engagements down through the history of the great controversy. But then Read went on to say:

> All through the ages Satan has warred against heaven. Now comes his final effort—his attempt to vanquish the government of the Most High. Into this blind obsession he pours all his hellish craftiness, his diabolical cunning, his malignant hatred; it is his supreme essay, his last desperate venture, to gain universal sway.
>
> There have been crises in the work of God before, but nothing like this crisis; there have been times of acute trouble through the centuries, but never a time of trouble like this one; there have been times of devastating, destructive war, but never such a time of utter abandonment, of universal carnage, of vindictive malignity, as now. To the evil one Armageddon is the grand culmination of all the pent-up passions of devilish spite and satanic bitterness. Now is seen the fullest fruition of his hellish design; now it is seen in all its naked enormity. It is stripped of its glamour and veneer; the principles of the archrebel are now unmasked, and can be seen by all the inhabitants in the great universe

of God in their true perspective.

The war of Armageddon is the summing up of all this remorseless opposition and violent hatred. Wars there have been throughout the centuries; nation has fought against nation all through earth's history. The kings of the earth have engaged in titanic struggles right up to the close of probation, but nothing up to that time could be called Armageddon.[4]

So, "nothing up to" "Satan's supreme essay," his "final effort . . . to vanquish the government of the Most High," "could be called Armageddon," yet, strangely, Armageddon is "a *series* of engagements rather than *one* conflict in this closing struggle." Read went on to stress the view that nothing before the last mighty struggle between good and evil, or the war on the saints, could be denominated Armageddon. This is how he put it:

The same applies to every other kind of conflict—the contest between good and evil, or the war against the saints. Nothing before this could be denominated Armageddon. But this last, mighty struggle is called by this name.[5]

Read continued:

We might suggest at least four great battles in this last mighty war:
a. There will be the battle between truth and error.
This involves the conflict between good and evil, between the law of God and the laws of men. . . .
b. There will be a battle against the saints.
Satan still continues his set purpose to obliterate the

people of God. . . .

c. There will be the battle of nation against nation.

This seems to take place after the voice of God is heard bringing deliverance to the saints. Then the leaders of men with the nations of earth, become so enraged, so infuriated, that their prey has been snatched from their grasp, that they turn and fight one another. . . .

d. Then there will be the battle when the Lord from heaven rides forth and has His controversy with the nations.

Then the kings of the earth, together with the beast and his armies, are arrayed against Christ the Lord. . . .

Now the sword of divine justice is unsheathed; now the artillery of heaven is brought into action. . . .

Of *this grand climax,* when the nations make war against Christ and are destroyed, we read:

"Jesus rides forth a mighty conqueror . . . 'faithful and true.' 'In righteousness he doth judge and make war.' And 'the armies which were in heaven follow him.' " [*The Great Controversy,* p. 641]

"At the coming of Christ the wicked are blotted from the face of the whole earth,—consumed with the spirit of His mouth, and destroyed by the brightness of His glory." [Ibid., p. 657.][6]

Read went on to say that, although Armageddon would be a contest between the forces of good and evil, there would also be a clash of nations, involving real combat. Said he:

However *spiritual* the conflict between good and evil may have been, it is nonetheless sure that the end of the conflict will mean *real* combat, *real* fire, *real* hailstones, and *real* destruction upon the nations. . . .[7]

This is how Read described the bloodbath resulting from this final clash of nations:

> This reign of carnage, of decimation, of slaughter, takes place after the voice of God is heard delivering His people from the hands of the wicked, and *before* the actual Advent of Christ, and is, we believe, part of the war of Armageddon.[8]

Elsewhere in his presentation, under the heading of *"Battle of the Nations,"* Read said:

> For many years, in fact, ever since the beginning of our work, we have taught that the battle of Armageddon, in some way or other, would involve the nations of earth in a final clash of arms. This position, we believe, is well sustained by the Word of God.[9]

That Seventh-day Adventists from the beginning of their work had taught that Armageddon in some way or other involved the nations in a final clash of arms is questionable, as the evidence shows, but apparently Read was unaware of this.

A few pages before, under the sidebar, *The Issues in the Final Conflict*, Read had said:

> It is evident that when the time comes for the final conflict there will be an agreement of some kind among the spirits of devils, the kings of the earth, and the leaders of men in various phases of endeavor. Satan ultimately succeeds in bringing about a confederation of all earth's interests, the great purpose of which is that he be exalted as divine. . . .

There is but one outcome to this effort, deceptive and diabolical as it is, and that is that "Satan is uniting his forces for perdition." In this final struggle Satan is bringing to a focus the same hostility to and contempt for the law of God that he has had from the beginning. The law of Jehovah is despised, the Sabbath of the commandments is disregarded, and a false institution is put in its place.[10]

So Armageddon would be "a harmony between the church and the world," in which "the Sabbath . . . is disregarded, and a false institution [Sunday] is put in its place," and this harmony between the church and the world would lead to "persecution of the saints . . . all over the world,"[11] culminating in an "international death decree."[12]

By saying on the one hand that Armageddon "involve[d] the nations in a final clash of arms," Read appears to have been attempting to pacify the "military Armageddonists." On the other hand, by saying that "Satan ultimately succeeds in bringing about a confederation of all of earth's interests," resulting in "an international death decree" against Sabbath keepers he appears to have been trying to satisfy the "spiritual Armageddonists." The following paragraph seems to make this clear:

From this review of the texts relating to the clash of nations, together with the comments from the Spirit of prophecy [*sic*], one might conclude that whatever conflict there might be between the nations—which could be part of the great war of Armageddon—comes after the voice of God has delivered the saints. Then the nations, together with religious leaders, are so chagrined and frustrated at seeing the children of God—those whom they had determined to obliterate from the face of the earth—now beyond

their reach that they turn and fight among themselves until
the earth itself literally rolls "in blood."[13]

The picture presented seems confusing. How does the "last
and final clash of" "nations" cause the wicked to fight each other
as the result of their being "chagrined and frustrated at seeing
the children of God . . . now beyond their reach"?

Be that as it may, by describing Armageddon as an international clash of arms, the military Armageddonists could claim
victory. On the other hand, by depicting the battle as a conflict
over the Sunday vs. Sabbath question, in which the nations issue
an international death decree against God's people, the spiritual
Armageddonists could claim victory. As a consequence, for years
after the conference, and perhaps even to this day, there are
Adventists who glibly say that Armageddon is both a spiritual as
well as a military battle of nations.

The Committee on Biblical Study and Research

Following the Bible Conference, the General Conference set
up the Committee on Biblical Study and Research to review the
church's traditional view of Armageddon. In a report in the March
1954 issue of *Ministry* magazine (pp. 22-27), the committee unani-
mously concluded that "Uriah Smith . . . reflected the popular
Protestant and secular viewpoint"[14] of Daniel 11:36-45 and the
committee reverted to the original Adventist view, that the power
referred to in verses 36-39 was "the Papacy."[15] At the same time
it considered verses 40-45 to be "largely unfulfilled prophecy"[16]
and cautioned against attempting to be dogmatic about the future
course of history "lest we assume the role of prophets ourselves."[17]

With respect to the identity of the last power of Daniel 11
mentioned in these latter verses, a majority of the members of
the committee believed that the "king of the north" and the "king

of the south" would yet "play their part in the final history within . . . the eastern Mediterranean,"[18] feeling "that these verses need to be studied in the light of present-day developments."[19] On the other hand, "some members" felt that Daniel 11 should be studied in connection with the 17th and 18th chapters of Revelation.[20]

Last Holdouts for the Military/Spiritual Views

Roy Allan Anderson and Jay Milton Hoffman were among the last holdouts for a mélange of the military as well as the spiritual views of the "war of Armageddon." In their book, *All Eyes on Israel* (1976), while describing Armageddon as "a war to the death between the forces of good and evil,"[21] they also described it as an armed conflict. Their view can probably be best described as a sanitized evangelical version of last-day events. Here is how they described the coming war of Armageddon:

"The land of Magog" was well understood by ancient historians. They state that the Magogites were divided into two distinct peoples—the European, known as Japhetic and the Asiatic, known as Turanian. The Greeks and the Romans spoke of the Japhetic race as Sarmatians, (not to be confused with Samaritans) [sic] of whom the Slavs are direct descendants. Some claim them to be a mixture of Medes and Scythians. Their region was originally that huge area north of the Black Sea, extending all the way from the Baltic to the Ural Mountains. The other group, the Turanians, known as the Asiatic Magogites or Scythians, were found in that great plateau in central Asia where the Tartars, the Cossacks, the Kalmaks and the Mongols are located today. This whole region was for centuries known as Muscovy.

Persia is the first country in the list mentioned in Ezekiel 38. This is present-day Iran. We might wonder why this land is introduced. A glance at the map will reveal how much easier it would be to move a large land army across the Elburz Mountains on the edge of Iran rather than attempting to cross the Caucasus Mountains that border Turkey.[22]

Gog, according to these authors, will be—

"the chief prince", who will appear in "the latter days". The Scripture calls him 'the prince of Rosh . . . in the land of Magog.' (See *New English Bible* and many other translations.) This leader named Gog seems destined to act as the commander-in-chief of a great confederacy. And according to the prophecy seems destined to make a vicious attack upon the land of Israel just before Christ's second coming.[23]

It seems clear that these writers were suggesting that the peoples comprising the former Soviet Union, led by Russia, would come through Iran, rather than over the Caucasus mountains, swing westward, cross the Tigris and Euphrates rivers, and attack Israel from the north. Armageddon would follow.

They continue developing this scenario:

The great super-powers in our world today [in 1975 the United States and the Soviet Union], while seeking to live in harmony with each other, are nevertheless, eyeing each other with deep concern. While encouraging progress toward peace is being made, yet it seems neither one is fully trustful of the other. Sometime before our Lord's return the Scripture indicates that a great peace movement will embrace the whole world and for a brief time the nations will "learn war no more." Outwardly it will appear genuine, but it will be the greatest deception the world has ever known.

The Apostle Paul warns God's people of this in 1 Thessalonians 5:1-8. Under the pretext of World Government and universal peace the nations will enter into an agreement on a scale hitherto undreamed of. It will appear that we have at last created a lasting peace.[24]

Anderson and Hoffman then tried to work Ellen White's description of Satan's impersonation of Christ into this scenario by asking:

> Could it be that the gathering of the nations to "the place called in the Hebrew tongue Armageddon" (Rev. 16:16) is the climax of a series of deceptions when Satan, appearing as "an angel of light" and impersonating Christ will himself declare he has come in fulfillment of our Lord's promise to return and bring universal peace? Are we prepared if Satan were to come as a great leader, teacher and benefactor?[25]

Just how Ellen White's statement that Satan, impersonating Christ and promoting Sunday observance, leads to Armageddon the authors do not make clear. What does seem to be clear is that "Gog [Russia] leads his aerial and cavalry invasion . . . [of] the Holy Land."[26]

But at this point the authors broaden the war of Armageddon to encompass, not merely Megiddo, but the entire planet. This is how they describe that war:

> "The Battle of the Great Day of God Almighty," at the end of the age when Christ returns described in Revelation 16:14 . . . will be more than a military affair in a little corner of southwestern Asia; it will be a world-wide struggle led by demons who will gather all the nations and lead them in a

war against God. It is not difficult to see this as the climax in the great controversy started by Lucifer long ago at the very headquarters of the universe. This conflict will not be confined to any one land. The issues are much larger than usually imagined. The Scriptures indicate that every land of earth will be involved. . . . Armageddon will be a demon-inspired revolt against God. . . .

Soon Satan will plunge the world into a holocaust of destruction far more terrible than that which swept over Jerusalem in A.D. 70. And this will not be confined to one city nor even to one nation for every country and every nation of the world will be involved. But at the height of the conflagration Christ Himself will appear leading forth the armies of heaven.[27]

So, appearing as an angel of light, Satan will bring about a universal false peace, and this false peace plunges the world into a holocaust of destruction, but how, the authors do not say.

Today, few Adventists espouse this view of Armageddon.

A Shift Toward the Spiritual View

During the twenty-five years following the 1952 Bible Conference there was a gradual shift away from the military concept of Armageddon and toward the spiritual view. Since about 1975 virtually all Adventists have believed that Armageddon is a spiritual battle over the Sabbath question. In other words, we appear to be coming full circle back to the interpretation held by the pioneers of the Advent message between 1847 and the mid-1860s. Most books and articles in the church's publications in recent years dealing with the subject clearly identify the combatants as apostate Protestantism, Roman Catholicism, and spiritualism,[28] with the focal issue being the seventh-day Sabbath vs. Sunday worship. As the conflict intensifies, the powers of earth issue a death decree, from which the voice of God delivers His beleaguered people at the last possible moment (*The Great Controversy,* pp. 635, 636).

Hans K. LaRondelle and Chariots of Salvation

Chariots of Salvation, by Hans K. La Rondelle, probably represents the most current Adventist view of Armageddon. A teacher at Andrews University for twenty-five years and now retired, he probably has helped more young ministers base their understanding of Armageddon on sound hermeneutic principles than anyone else in the church. This is how he interprets Revelation 16:12-16:

> Armageddon will differ from its types in the Old Testament in that the entire world population will divide into those who are the new-covenant people of God and those who are their decided enemies.

Armageddon in Its Apocalyptic Context

Then I saw three evil spirits that looked like frogs; they came out of the mouth of the dragon, out of the mouth of the beast and out of the mouth of the false prophet. They are the spirits of demons performing miraculous signs, and they go out to the kings of the whole world, to gather them for the battle on the great day of God Almighty.

"Behold. I come like a thief! Blessed is he who stays awake and keeps his clothes with him, so that he may not go naked and be shamefully exposed."

Then they gathered the kings together to the place

that in Hebrew is called Armageddon (Rev. 16:13-16).

This section records a distinct vision . . . that seems to interrupt the flow of the sixth and seventh plagues. We may understand the interlude as a description of how the demonic spirits prepare the world for the final war of God. Subsequent visions explain more specifically that Armageddon is the final showdown between end-time Babylon and the Messiah (see Rev. 17:14 and 19:11-21).

John saw three evil spirits emerge from the dragon, the beast, and the false prophet. Mounce explains that "the unclean spirits proceed from the *mouths* of the unholy triumvirate, suggesting the persuasive and deceptive propaganda which in the last days will lead men to an unconditional commitment to the cause of evil" (*The Book of Revelation,* p. 299).

Left unanswered is the question: What actually is this universal "cause of evil"? The text says, "Go out to the kings of the whole world *[oikoumen]* to gather them for the battle on the great day of God Almighty" (verse 14). Some have jumped to the conclusion that the words predict a world war between an Eastern and a Western block of nations. Such a speculation can rise only when one first dissects the words of Scripture completely from their biblical root and context. No war between nation and nation is in view here. The climax of John's Apocalypse deals with far more serious evil in God's sight: apostate religious forces will lead all political powers on earth to unite for one common cause, waging war against God's people! . . . The fact that Christ's people will be at the center of the apocalyptic war we can infer already from Christ's warning:

Behold, I come like a thief! Blessed is he who stays

awake and keeps his clothes with him, so that he may not go naked and be shamefully exposed (Rev. 16:15).

Christ summons His followers hereby to stay spiritually awake and to be prepared for the critical moment at the end of history. Only when the believer in Christ is clad spiritually in the garment of Christ's righteousness can he stand firm in the final test of faith (cf. Rev. 3:18). . . .

The demon-inspired union of all political and apostate religious powers on earth turns against the faithful people of Christ. We can see its meaning only in the light of the cosmic war between God and Satan, between Christ and His antichrist. . . . The ultimate issue is Who will rule the universe? . . . Fallen angels constantly gather or unite political and military leaders for one ultimate goal, the destruction of Christ's church. "They will make war against the Lamb, but the Lamb will overcome them because he is Lord of lords and King of kings—and with him will be his called, chosen and faithful followers" (Rev. 17:14). . . .

But how in reality do the kings of the earth "wage war" against the Lamb of God? George B. Caird explains, "The only way in which earthly kings can wage war on the Lamb is through his followers. The war is therefore yet another reference to the great persecution" (*The Revelation of St. John the Divine* [New York: Harper and Row, 1966], p. 220). . . .

John's vision about Armageddon in Revelation 19 fully discloses God's response to the satanic plot aimed at the people of Christ. Here the revelator portrays Christ as the celestial warrior, riding on His white battle horse, who will come to the rescue of His people.

I saw heaven standing open and there before me

was a white horse, whose rider is called Faithful and True. With justice he judges and makes war. His eyes are like blazing fire, and on his head are many crowns. He has a name written on him that no one but he himself knows. He is dressed in a robe dipped in blood, and his name is the Word of God. The armies of heaven were following him, riding on white horses and dressed in fine linen, white and clean. Out of his mouth comes a sharp sword with which to strike down the nations. "He will rule them with an iron scepter." He treads the winepress of the fury of the wrath of God Almighty. On his robe and on his thigh he has this name written:

KING OF KINGS AND LORD OF LORDS. . . .

Then I saw the beast and the kings of the earth and their armies gathered together to make war against the rider on the horse and his army (Rev. 19:11-19).

This vision of the second advent of Christ proclaims that He comes both to rescue His church and to execute the Messianic judgment on the wicked. . . .

John's apocalyptic vision of Christ as divine judge and warrior transforms Yahweh's judgment against the enemies of Israel into a judgment by Christ against the enemies of *His* people. Israel's enemies become "the beast and the kings of the earth" and "the false prophet" (Rev. 19:19, 20). During Armageddon Christ will be a refuge for His people, a stronghold for the Israel of God, wherever they are in the world.[29]

Farther along LaRondelle writes:

Armageddon is Heaven's response to the cries of the Israel of God for deliverance from the Babylonian oppressor. The Apocalypse presents only two contrasting armies in the confrontation at Armageddon. On the one hand are "the kings of the whole world" who follow apostate religious authorities and spirits of demons (Rev. 16:14), while on the other hand are "the kings from the East" (verse 12), who come to bring judgment on this universal conspiracy against the Israel of God. The two opposing kinds of "kings" have led many Bible expositors to the conviction that "the kings from the East" do not belong to the Babylonian world but are rather celestial redeemers of God's people.[30]

LaRondelle says concerning mystical Babylon of the end-time:

What happened to the ancient city [of Babylon] gives us clues to the fate of evil and its supporters during the days before Christ's second coming.[31]

John the revelator takes his motif for Revelation 16:12-16 from the capture of Babylon by Cyrus the Great. Says LaRondelle:

Babylon . . . collapsed when (according to historical tradition) the Persian general Cyrus suddenly diverted the northern inflow of the Euphrates . . . , to a nearby lake so that his soldiers could enter Babylon by way of the dry riverbed.[32]

Exegetes have observed that the description of the *sixth* plague—the sudden drying up of the great river Euphrates (verse 12)—merely announces the *preparation* of the political powers for the actual battle of Armageddon. The Armageddon clash itself we would therefore expect to occur during the seventh plague. But all we hear for the final plague is that Babylon the great collapses and is destroyed (verse 19). Armageddon and the destruction of universal Babylon are therefore identical. We may recognize in the unity of the sixth and the seventh plagues two consecutive stages of the Armageddon event: the preliminary drying up of the great river Euphrates and the subsequent fall of Babylon the great.[33]

LaRondelle interprets the several symbols associated with the sixth and seventh plagues as follows:

Babylon: functioned as the enemy of Yahweh and the oppressor of Israel.

Euphrates: as an integral part of Babylon, it supported the capital as a protective wall, thus it was likewise hostile to Israel.

Drying Up of the Euphrates: as Yahweh's judgment on Babylon, it caused her sudden downfall and functioned as the initiation of Israel's deliverance.

Cyrus as general of the kings of the Medes and the Persians: Yahweh "anointed" Cyrus in order to defeat Babylon and set Israel free. Cyrus and the kings from the east were thus the enemies of Babylon and deliverers of Israel.[34]

This is how he elaborates on the drying up of the Euphrates:

The apocalyptic drying up of Babylon's river . . . suggests God's final judgment on Babylon (Rev. 16:12). In reality this judgment will occur when the civil multitudes of all nations suddenly realize God has weighed and sentenced religious Babylon. Then they will at once withdraw their allegiance, even reversing their once loyal support into such active hate that they completely destroy Babylon.[35]

LaRondelle identifies the dragon in these words:

[John] identifies the dragon with "that ancient serpent called the devil or Satan" ([Rev. 12] verse 9), a direct reference to the serpent who deceived man in Paradise, according to the first book of the Bible.

This inspired connection between the dragon of the last days with humanity's deceiver in Paradise indicates that Satan's last struggle against mankind is basically of the same religious nature as the first conflict in the Garden of Eden. . . . Always he has been suggesting that the word of God is untrustworthy, that God's moral law is too restrictive of human freedom—as it denies us absolute autonomy—and therefore must be changed, and that God's penalty of death for the transgressor is not true because death means only the transition to a higher sphere of life and wisdom (see Gen 3:1-4; Dan. 7:25). This great delusion will only increase and reach its climax in the time of the end.[36]

Satan's twofold, latter-day lies are, therefore, that God's law needs alteration and that the penalty for the transgression of that law is not death but a transition to a higher state of existence. This latter belief is a basic tenet of spiritism.

As for the identity of the Babylonian beast, LaRondelle quotes approvingly J. Myssingberde Ford, who says that

the harlot Babylon of the book of Revelation designates not the Roman Empire but a perverted "Jerusalem," "faithless

Israel," of the Christian Era ([J. M. Ford, *Revelation,*] pp. 282-288).[37]

LaRondelle quotes Ford further as saying that it refers to

a religious apostasy of universal magnitude within Christendom.[38]

This leaves little doubt as to the identity of the earth beast of the unholy triumvirate of Revelation 16:13. Elsewhere LaRondelle identifies Babylon as "Roman Christianity." Time, he indicates, will clarify the identity of the beast with the lamblike horns, which the revelator also called the false prophet (cf. Rev. 16:13; 19:20; 13:11-17).

---

1. A. V. Olson, "The Place of Prophecy in Our Preaching," *Our Firm Foundation* (Hagerstown, Md.: Review and Herald Publishing Association, 1953), vol. 2, p. 547. (abbrev. *OFF*).
2. *OFF,* vol. 2, p. 305.
3. Ibid., p. 306. Italics his.
4. Ibid., p. 307.
5. Ibid., p. 307.
6. Ibid., pp. 307-310. Emphasis his.
7. Ibid., p. 310. Emphasis his.
8. Ibid., p. 303. Emphasis his.
9. Ibid., p. 297.
10. Ibid., pp. 262-264.
11. Ibid., p. 295.
12. Ibid., p. 271.
13. Ibid., p. 304.
14. *Ministry,* March 1954, p. 24.
15. Ibid., pp. 24, 25.
16. Ibid., p. 26.
17. Ibid., p. 27.
18. Ibid., p. 26.
19. Ibid.

20. Ibid.

21. Roy Allan Anderson and Jay Milton Hoffman, *All Eyes on Israel* (Fort Worth, Tex.: McElhaney Printing & Publishing Company, 1976), p. 197.

22. Ibid., p. 210.

23. Ibid., p. 202.

24. Ibid., p. 217,

25. Ibid., pp. 217, 218.

26. Ibid., p. 215.

27. Ibid., pp. 220, 221, 223.

28. *The Great Controversy,* pp. 588, 589.

29. Hans K. LaRondelle, *Chariots of Salvation* (Hagerstown, Md.: Review and Herald Publishing Association, 1987), pp. 124-128.

30. Ibid., p. 144.

31. Ibid., p. 91.

32. Ibid., p. 94.

33. Ibid., pp. 99, 100.

34. Ibid., p. 102.

35. Ibid., pp. 103, 104.

36. Ibid., pp. 147, 148.

37. Ibid., p. 152.

38. Ibid., p. 153.

RETURN TO THE ORIGINAL ADVENTIST VIEW

As mentioned in chapter 6, it was the serious study of the writings of Ellen White, which began in the 1920s, that in time led to a re-study of Daniel 11 and Revelation 16 in light of the Spirit of Prophecy writings. This has led to a return, or near return, to the original Seventh-day Adventist views on Armageddon and the last power of Daniel 11. Time will probably see a complete return to the original view.

While the Spirit of Prophecy's views of eschatology differed significantly from the views expressed by Uriah Smith, which the church largely adopted after James White's death, Ellen White never quarreled with Smith over these differences—nor did he quarrel with her over her views. To the contrary, Smith seems to have seen no inconsistency between his views of the nations fighting against each other and Ellen White's depiction of all nations uniting to persecute God's remnant people and issuing a worldwide death decree against them. That Smith saw no inconsistency between his eschatological views and Ellen White's description of last-day events is made evident in the third volume of Arthur White's biography of his grandmother, in which he says:

> Uriah Smith was on the grounds [of the Portland, Maine, camp meeting], and . . . [on the evening of September 10, 1884, Ellen White] shared with him some of the page proofs, just received, for *The Great Controversy.* He was deeply moved in reading the chapter on "The Time of Trouble" and felt every sentence of it was needed.[1]

Even though the majority of Adventists adopted Smith's views of Armageddon and the king of the north rather than those of James White, his wife showed no resentment. On the contrary, she gave unstinting praise for Smith's *D&R,* because it contained "precious instruction,"[2] and she urged Adventist canvassers to sell it, for it had "been the means of bringing many precious souls to a knowledge of the truth."[3]

By endorsing *D&R* Ellen White did not mean that she agreed with everything in Smith's book. For example, she obviously did not endorse Smith's interpretation of Revelation 3:14, in which he says that Christ "came into existence" at some time in eternity past,[4] whereas she taught, clearly and unequivocally, that Christ has "existed from eternity."[5] What she was apparently endorsing was the fact that *D&R* upheld the landmarks of the SDA message[6]—the cleansing of the heavenly sanctuary, the three angels' messages of Revelation 14, the perpetuity of God's law, the Second Coming, and the nonimmortality of the soul,[7] as well as the prophetic time periods.[8]

On the other hand, as has earlier been pointed out in this book, although Ellen White was well aware that her husband

and Uriah Smith did not see eye to eye on the identity of the last power of Daniel 11, she never made an issue of this matter. Obviously, it was not a teaching vital to Seventh-day Adventism.

When the Books of Daniel and Revelation Are Better Understood

Concerning the biblical books, Daniel and the Revelation, Ellen White says:

> In the past teachers have declared Daniel and the Revelation to be sealed books, and the people have turned [away] from them. . . . Revelation means that something of importance is revealed. . . .
>
> This book demands close, prayerful study, lest it be interpreted according to the ideas of men, and false construction be given to the sacred word of the Lord, which in its symbols and figures means so much to us. There is so much that we positively must understand in order that we may shape our course of action so that we shall not receive the plagues which are coming upon the world. . . .
>
> When the books of Daniel and Revelation are better understood, believers will have an entirely different religious experience. They will be given such glimpses of the open gates of heaven that heart and mind will be impressed in regard to the character all must develop in order to realize the blessedness which is to be the reward of the pure in heart.[9]

This statement teaches that if the book of Revelation is "interpreted according to the ideas of men," it will be given a "false construction." The same, of course, would be true of the book of Daniel. Ellen White then looks forward to the time when God's remnant people "will have an entirely different religious experience" as a result of having a better understanding of these prophetic books.

Most everyone will admit that there is nothing particularly spiritual about an Armageddon that consists of a bloody battle of nations in the Middle East or Turkey being driven from Europe and setting up its capital in Jerusalem. However, seeing Armageddon and the activity of the revived papal power as aspects of the cosmic conflict between the forces of good and evil can produce "an entirely different religious experience." This is something to ponder.

Ellen White's View of Armageddon

Ellen White had much to say about "Armageddon"—"the battle of that great day of God Almighty." Besides these terms, she also speaks of this conflict as "the battle of the great day," "the last great battle," "the last great warfare," "the last great contest," "the last conflict," etc.

Speaking regarding to the nature of this battle, she says:

In this last conflict the Captain of the Lord's host is leading on the armies of heaven, and mingling in the ranks and fighting our battles for us. We shall have apostasies; we expect them. . . .

Notice that while the "last conflict" is described in military terms, it has to do with "apostasies." Ellen White continues:

The angel, the mighty angel from heaven, is to lighten the earth with his glory, while he cries mightily with a loud voice, "Babylon the great is fallen, is fallen" (Rev. 18:2). . . . We would lose faith and courage in the conflict if we were not sustained by the power of God.

The "mighty angel"—the angel of Revelation 18:2—mentioned here is elsewhere closely associated with the latter rain.[10] Ellen White continues:

> Every form of evil is to spring into intense activity. Evil angels unite their powers with evil men, and as they have been in constant conflict and attained an experience in the best modes of deception and battle, and have been strengthening for centuries, they will not yield the last great final contest without a desperate struggle. All the world will be on one side or the other of the question.
>
> The Battle of Armageddon will be fought, and that day must find none of us sleeping. Wide-awake we must be, as wise virgins having oil in our vessels with our lamps. . . . The power of the Holy Ghost must be upon us, and the Captain of the Lord's host will stand at the head of the angels of heaven to direct the battle.

There will only be two sides in "Armageddon"—"evil angels" united with "evil men", versus "the Captain of the Lord's host" "at the head of the angels of heaven" and those who are on His side (Rev. 17:14)—His remnant on earth. The statement continues:

> Solemn events before us are yet to transpire. Trumpet after trumpet is to be sounded; vial after vial poured out one after another upon the inhabitants of the earth. Scenes of stupendous interest are right upon us and these things will be sure indications of the presence of Him who has directed in every aggressive movement, [the One] who has accompanied the march of His cause through all the ages, and who has graciously pledged Himself to be with His people in all their conflicts to the end of the world. He will

vindicate His truth. He will cause it to triumph. He is ready to supply His faithful ones with motives and power of purpose, inspiring them with hope and courage and valor in increased activity as the time is at hand.

In spite of the "solemn events before us," we have the assurance that God "will vindicate His truth." The statement continues:

Deceptions, delusions, impostures will increase. The cries will come in from every quarter, "Lo, here is Christ! Lo, there is Christ!" "But," said Christ, "Go ye not after them" [Luke 21:8. See Matt. 24:23]. There will be one fierce struggle before the man of sin shall be disclosed to this world, who he is and what has been his work.

While the Protestant world is becoming very tender and affectionate toward the man of sin [2 Thess. 2:3], shall [not] God's people take their place as bold and valiant soldiers of Jesus Christ, to meet the issue which must come, their lives hid with Christ in God? Mystic Babylon has not been sparing in the blood of the saints, and shall we [not] be wide-awake to catch the beams of light which have been shining from the light of the angel who is to brighten the earth with his glory?[11]

Today we see "the Protestant world" making just such overtures to the "man of sin"—the papacy—as here described.

Ellen White's statement makes it clear that Armageddon is a battle over spiritual issues and that it is related to the descent of the angel of Revelation 18. The importance of this connection will be seen in the next statement. She says:

John in the Revelation writes of the unity of those living on the earth to make void the law of God. "These have one mind, and shall give their power and strength unto the beast. These shall make war with the Lamb, and the Lamb shall overcome them: for He is Lord of lords, and King of kings: and they that are with him are called, and chosen, and faithful" (Revelation 17:13, 14). "And I saw three unclean spirits like frogs come out of the mouth of the dragon, and out of the mouth of the beast, and out of the mouth of the false prophet" (Revelation 16:13). All who will exalt and worship the idol sabbath, a day that God has not blessed, help the devil and his angels with all the power of their God-given ability, which they have perverted to a wrong use. Inspired by another spirit which blinds their discernment, they cannot see that the exaltation of Sunday observance is entirely the institution of the [Roman] Catholic church.

Observe that the deceptive activity of the three unclean spirits of Revelation 16:13 is related to "the exaltation of Sunday observance"—"the institution of the [Roman] Catholic church." The statement continues:

A period is coming when everyone will take sides between the Sabbath of the fourth commandment, which the Lord has sanctified and blessed, and the spurious sabbath instituted by the man of sin.... And as Nebuchadnezzar, the king of Babylon, issued a decree that all who would not bow down and worship this image should be killed, so a proclamation will be made that all who will not reverence the Sunday institution will be punished with imprisonment and death. Thus the Sabbath of the Lord is trampled underfoot. ...

The world is in co-partnership with the professed Christian churches in making void the law of Jehovah.

God's law is set aside; it is trampled underfoot; and from all the loyal people of God the prayer will ascend to heaven, "It is time, O Lord, for Thee to work: for they have made void Thy law" [Psalm 119:126]. Satan is making his last and most powerful effort for the mastery, his last conflict against the principles of God's law. A defiant infidelity abounds.

The issue in this coming conflict is "the Sabbath of the fourth commandment . . . [versus] the spurious sabbath instituted by the man of sin." (For a further discussion of this conflict, see my book *The Shape of the Coming Crisis*.) Ellen White continues:

After John's description in Revelation 16[:13, 14] of that miracle-working power which was to gather the world to the last great conflict, the symbols are dropped, and the trumpet voice once more gives a certain sound. "Behold, I come as a thief. Blessed is he that watcheth, and keepeth his garments, lest he walk naked, and they see his shame" [Revelation 16:15]."[12]

The fact that in Rev. 16:15 the symbols are dropped implies that the verses preceding and following this passage are symbolic, whereas verse 15 is not, in the usual sense of the term. In Letter 141, 1902, Ellen White quotes this verse and inserts in brackets a clarifying phrase, so that the verse reads: "Behold, I come as a thief. Blessed is he that keepeth his garments, lest he walk naked,—without the robe of Christ's righteousness—and they see his shame." This clarifying phrase gives a spiritual meaning to Revelation 16:15.

The Use of Military Terms for a Spiritual Conflict

Although Ellen White uses military terms to describe the coming conflict, this battle is clearly a spiritual struggle over spiritual issues. But notice how she uses martial terminology in her descriptions:

> Satan himself stands at the head of his army, striving with all his power to perfect the force over which he rules, that he may wreak his vengeance on God's people. Knowing that his time is short, he has come down with great power, to work against all that is good. . . .
>
> A terrible conflict is before us. We are nearing the battle of the great day of God Almighty. That which has been held in control is to be let loose. The angel of mercy is folding her wings, preparing to step down from the throne, and leave the world to the control of Satan.
>
> The principalities and powers of earth are in bitter revolt against the God of heaven. They are filled with hatred against those who serve him, and soon, very soon, will be fought the last great battle between good and evil. The earth is to be the battlefield—the scene of the final contest and the final victory. Here, where for so long Satan has led men against God, rebellion is to be forever suppressed.[13]

Again notice the following description of Armageddon in military terms:

> There are only two parties in our world, those who are loyal to God, and those who stand under the banner of the prince of darkness. Satan and his angels will come down with power and signs and lying wonders to deceive those who dwell on the earth, and if possible the very elect. The crisis is right upon us. Is this to paralyze the energies of those who have a knowledge of the truth? Is the influence of the powers of deception so far reaching that the influ-

ence of the truth will be overpowered?

The battle of Armageddon is soon to be fought. He on whose vesture is written the name, King of kings and Lord of lords, leads forth the armies of heaven on white horses, clothed in fine linen, clean and white.[14]

In the foregoing statement Ellen White clearly uses military language to describe a spiritual conflict. She does the same in the next statement:

The present is a solemn, fearful time for the church. The angels are already girded, awaiting the mandate of God to pour their vials of wrath upon the world. Destroying angels are taking up the work of vengeance; for the Spirit of God is gradually withdrawing from the world. Satan is also mustering his forces of evil, going forth "unto the kings of the earth and of the whole world," to gather them under his banner, to be trained for "the battle of that great day of God Almighty" [Rev. 16:13]. Satan is to make most powerful efforts for the mastery in the last great conflict. Fundamental principles will be brought out, and decisions made in regard to them.[15]

The Issue in the Battle: The Sabbath Commandment of God's Law

According to Ellen White, the central issue in Armageddon is spiritual, although she couches this conflict in military terms:

The Master is binding the precious grain in bundles for the heavenly garner, while the wicked are gathering together as fagots for the fires of the last day. The church and the world are preparing for the last great contest, in which all must act a part. The kingdoms of the whole world are gathering their forces to the battle of the great day, when the wrath of God will be manifested against the nations that have made void his law.[16]

It is on [the question of] the law of God that the last great struggle of the controversy between Christ and His angels and Satan and his angels will come, and it will be decisive for all the world. . . .

Men in responsible positions will not only ignore and despise the Sabbath themselves, but from the sacred desk, will urge upon the people the observance of the first day of the week, pleading tradition and custom in behalf of this man-made institution.[17]

So, although the coming conflict is described in military terms, it is clearly spiritual in nature; specifically, it is over the Sabbath commandment of God's law.

When Armageddon Begins and Ends

The Spirit of Prophecy tells us when Armageddon commences and when it ends:

Satan's agents have not been sparing of the blood of the saints. Christ's true followers are kind, tender, pitiful. They will realize the meaning of the work of the angel of Revelation 18, who is to lighten the whole earth with his glory, while he cries with a loud voice, "Babylon the great is fallen, is fallen" [verse 2]. Many will heed this call.

We need to study the pouring out of the seventh vial. The powers of evil will not yield up the conflict without a struggle. But Providence has a part to act in the battle of Armageddon. When the earth is lighted with the glory of the angel of Revelation 18, the religious elements, good and evil, will awake from slumber, and the armies of the living God will take the field.[18]

The descent of the angel of Revelation 18 symbolizes the outpouring of the latter rain—an event that clearly takes place *before* the close of probation.[19] Thus Armageddon begins *before* probation closes, for the simple reason that the battle is joined "when the earth is lighted with the glory of the angel of Revelation 18." The battle ends *when* "the seventh vial" is poured out on the wicked and God intervenes to deliver His people.

The Sixth Plague

The sixth plague is clearly not Armageddon. As previously pointed out, the sixth vial is the drying up of the symbolic Euphrates, yet Armageddon is related to this plague. Not only this, but the battle is not fought under the sixth vial; rather, the gathering of the forces of evil reaches its critical climax under this plague. God's intervention in the battle occurs under the seventh vial when the forces of evil are routed. This is why "we need to study the pouring out of the seventh vial," for "Providence [God] has a part to act in the battle." God enters the conflict when His voice delivers His people from their enemies during the seventh plague.[20]

War in the Last Days

Does this mean that there will be no armed conflicts in the last days? No. According to Ellen White, there will be wars. She says:

> In the last scenes of this earth's history, war will rage. There will be pestilence, plague, and famine. The waters of the deep will overflow their boundaries. Property and life will be destroyed by fire and flood.[21]

However, when Ellen White says that in the final scenes of earth's history war will rage, she is usually speaking of spiritual warfare. Thus there will doubtless be wars between nations in the last days, but the important point is that she never calls such warfare Armageddon. In describing the mutual slaughter of the wicked in the last scenes of this earth's history (*GC,* p. 642), she simply speaks of "the clash of arms, the tumult of battle, 'with confused noise, and garments rolled in blood.' " Observe also that this occurs *after* the seventh plague.

Deadly Instruments of Warfare Invented for Armageddon
There is one Spirit of Prophecy statement, however, that seems to teach that Armageddon is an armed conflict of nations:

> Four mighty angels hold back the powers of this earth till the servants of God are sealed in their foreheads. The nations of the world are eager for conflict; but they are held in check by the angels. When this restraining power is removed, there will come a time of trouble and anguish. Deadly instruments of warfare will be invented. Vessels, with their living cargo, will be entombed in the great deep. All who have not the spirit of truth will unite under the leadership of satanic agencies. But they are to be kept under control till the time shall come for the great battle of Armageddon.
>
> Angels are belting the world, refusing Satan his claims to supremacy, made because of the vast multitude of his adherents. We hear not the voices, we see not with the natural sight the work of these angels, but their hands are linked about the world, and with sleepless vigilance they are keeping the armies of Satan at bay till the sealing of God's people shall be accomplished.[22]

What is described here is clearly a spiritual conflict. Yet into it Ellen White injects what appears to be literal language: "Deadly instruments of warfare will be invented. Vessels, with their living cargo, will be entombed in the great deep." Is it possible that these seemingly literal expressions actually refer to spiritual things? The answer is Yes.

> Hatred against the law of God has continued to increase in intensity. Men have beaten one of the messengers of God, and killed another, and stoned another. New methods are continually devised to turn men away from the truth. The materials for the last great warfare are collecting; already the conflict has reached large proportions. And as iniquity abounds, the love of many waxes cold.[23]

The weapons in this statement clearly refer to abounding iniquity, not abundant military hardware. Thus the deadly instruments of warfare in the foregoing statement refer to the spiritual weapons of the evil one, not munitions of war.

But how do vessels with their living cargo being entombed in the great deep relate to a spiritual Armageddon? This way: When calamities occur, such as when "thousands of ships . . . [are] hurled into the depths of the sea," and "navies . . . go down,"[24] Sabbath keepers will be blamed for these calamities, because they refuse to keep Sunday.[25]

Thus, abounding iniquity and great catastrophes, which are blamed on the righteous, prepare the world for Armageddon, but these calamities are not Armageddon. They are the winds that Ellen White says are "kept under control *till* the time shall come for the great battle of Armageddon" (emphasis supplied).

Thus, before the time comes for Armageddon there may yet be

a great war in the Middle East. It may even center at Megiddo or the Valley of Jehoshaphat, but *it will not be the Armageddon of the Bible and the Spirit of Prophecy.* It will simply be armed conflict among the nations, concerning which Christ spoke of in Matthew 24.

The Drying up of the Euphrates and Babylon's Capture Are Symbolic

In her writings, Ellen White speaks of the capture of ancient Babylon by Cyrus by drying up the waters of the Euphrates as symbolic of the destruction of the world. Here is her statement:

> The destruction of Babylon pictures to some degree the final destruction of the world, of which the prophet writes, "Behold, the day of the Lord cometh, cruel both with wrath and fierce anger, to lay the land desolate; and he shall destroy the sinners thereof out of it." [Isa. 13:9.] Destruction came upon Babylon while the king and his lords were engaged in feasting and revelry. Cyrus and his army marched up the bed of the river Euphrates; for trenches had been dug, and the river turned from its course, so that there was no obstruction to their entering the city, provided the gates were opened. The guardsmen were indulging in merriment and revelry, and the city was left without defense. Before the officers were aware, the enemy had entered the city, and escape was impossible.[26]

And again, she says:

> To the ruler of Babylon came the sentence of the divine Watcher: O king, "to thee it is spoken; The kingdom is departed from thee." [Daniel 4:31.]
>
> "Come down, and sit in the dust, O virgin daughter of Babylon,

Sit on the ground: there is no throne. . . .
Sit thou silent,
And get thee into darkness, O daughter of the Chaldeans;
For thou shalt no more be called, The lady of kingdoms."
[Isa. 47:1-5.]

"O thou that dwellest upon many waters, abundant in
treasures,
Thine end is come." . . .
[Jer. 51:13.][27]

In *ST,* Dec. 29, 1890, Cyrus is referred to in connection with the
fall of ancient Babylon, which is symbolic of the end of the world. In
the book of Isaiah God calls Cyrus, who captured Babylon, "the
righteous man from the east," and in Isaiah 45:1, God promises "to
open before him the two leaved gates" of Babylon.

Cyrus the Great is a type of Christ. Darius the Mede, who
conquered Babylon with Cyrus (Dan. 5:31), represents the Father. At His second coming Christ comes not only accompanied
by all the angels of heaven but with His Father. Note that Christ
comes "with his own glory, and with the glory of the Father."[28]
The fact that the Father's glory accompanies the Son implies that
He comes with the Son, although He is not the main focus of
attention. (See 1 Cor. 15:23-28, TEV.) These, then, are the "kings
of the east" spoken of in Revelation 16:12. It seems unlikely that
the saints, who are allies of Christ (see Rev. 17:14), are included
as kings of the east, for they do not come from the east at the
Second Coming. Rather, *they are on earth* and see Christ and His
Father, the Kings of the east, *coming from the east.*[29]

The Seven Last Plagues
Let us now turn our attention to the sequence during the

seven last plagues and focus especially on the sixth. *The Great Controversy,* pages 627, 628 describes the first four plagues in these words:

> When Christ ceases His intercession in the [heavenly] sanctuary, the unmingled wrath threatened against those who worship the beast and his image and receive his mark (Rev. 14:9, 10), will be poured out. The plagues upon Egypt when God was about to deliver Israel were similar in character to those more terrible and extensive judgments which are to fall upon the world just before the final deliverance of God's people. Says the revelator, in describing those terrific scourges: "There fell a noisome and grievous sore upon the men which had the mark of the beast, and upon them which worshiped his image." The sea "became as the blood of a dead man: and every living soul died in the sea." And "the rivers and fountains of waters . . . became blood." Terrible as these inflictions are, God's justice stands fully vindicated. The angel of God declares: "Thou art righteous, O Lord, . . . because Thou hast judged thus. For they have shed the blood of saints and prophets, and Thou hast given them blood to drink; for they are worthy." Rev. 16:2-6. By condemning the people of God to death, they have as truly incurred the guilt of their blood as if it had been shed by their hands.

The third plague is clearly linked to the death decree. The statement continues:

> In the [fourth] plague that follows, power is given to the sun "to scorch men with fire. And men were scorched with great heat." Verses 8, 9. . . .
> These [first four] plagues are not universal, or the inhabit-

ants of the earth would be wholly cut off. Yet they will be the most awful scourges that have ever been known to mortals.[30]

The fact that the first four plagues are *not* universal implies that the last three *are,* and as it turns out, this conclusion is correct. The outpouring of the last three vials are described as follows:

> With shouts of triumph, jeering, and imprecation, throngs of evil men are about to rush upon their prey, when, lo, a dense blackness, deeper than the darkness of the night, falls upon the earth.

This is the fifth plague. The fact that the darkness of this plague falls upon the earth implies that it is worldwide—universal, unlike the first four plagues. It is evident, therefore, that by this time "the seat of the beast" (Rev. 15:10) includes the entire planet. The statement continues:

> Then a rainbow, shining with the glory from the throne of God, spans the heavens and seems to encircle each praying company. The angry multitudes are suddenly arrested. Their mocking cries die away. The objects of their murderous rage are forgotten. With fearful forebodings they gaze upon the symbol of God's covenant, and long to be shielded from its overpowering brightness.

This is clearly the sixth plague, for it is preceded by the fifth plague, and the statement continues with a description of the seventh plague—the mighty earthquake and the hailstorm:

> It is at midnight that God manifests His power for the deliverance of His people. The sun appears, shining in its

strength. Signs and wonders follow in quick succession. The wicked look with terror and amazement upon the scene, while the righteous behold with solemn joy the tokens of their deliverance. Everything in nature seems turned out of its course. The streams cease to flow. Dark, heavy clouds come up and clash against each other. In the midst of the angry heavens is one clear space of indescribable glory, whence comes the voice of God like the sound of many waters, saying: "It is done." Rev. 16:17.

That voice shakes the heavens and the earth. There is a mighty earthquake, "such as was not since men were upon the earth, so mighty an earthquake, and so great." Verses 17, 18. The firmament appears to open and shut. The glory from the throne of God seems flashing through. The mountains shake like a reed in the wind, and ragged rocks are scattered on every side. There is a roar as of a coming tempest. The sea is lashed into fury. There is heard the shriek of a hurricane, like the voice of demons upon a mission of destruction. *The whole earth* heaves and swells like the waves of the sea. Its surface is breaking up. Its very foundations seem to be giving way. Mountain chains are sinking. Inhabited islands disappear.... Great hailstones, every one "about the weight of a talent," are doing their work of destruction. [31]

This is the seventh plague—and it, too, is universal.

The symbolic Euphrates—the people supporting mystical Babylon (Rev. 17:15)—begins drying up when the "rainbow, shining with the glory from the throne of God" appears over each praying company and the wicked "are suddenly arrested." The voice of God is now heard, completing the drying up of the Euphrates. Says Ellen White:

When the voice of God turns the captivity of His people, there is a terrible awakening of those who have lost all in the great conflict of life. . . . Now . . . [the great men] are stripped of all that made them great, and are left destitute and defenseless. . . . The people see that they have been deluded. . . . The multitudes are filled with fury. . . . The swords which were to slay God's people are now employed to destroy their enemies. Everywhere there is strife and bloodshed.[32]

This is a literal description of what happens when the symbolic Euphrates dries up. The waters, representing people (Rev. 17:15) withdraw their support from spiritual Babylon. This is why, when the seventh plague is poured out, "the great city . . . [Babylon is] divided into three parts." In other words, the threefold union of apostate Protestantism, spiritualism, and Roman Catholicism (see *GC,* p. 588; *5T,* p. 451) is shattered.

The "clash of arms" described in *GC,* pp. 654-656, is not nation fighting nation but chaotic carnage—the wicked blaming each other for being lost and butchering each other with weapons intended to slay the saints. Thus while the issues in Armageddon are clearly spiritual, there is a physicial aspect to the battle—the wicked slay each other.

The King of the North of Daniel Eleven

We turn now to what Ellen White has to say about Daniel 11. She wrote only three comments regarding this chapter. Here are her statements:

The judgments of God are in the land. The wars and rumors of wars, the destruction by fire and flood, say clearly that the time of trouble, which is to increase until the end, is very near at hand. We have no time to lose. The world is stirred with the spirit of war. The prophecies of the eleventh [chapter] of Daniel have almost reached their final fulfil[l]ment.[33]

The prophecy of the eleventh chapter of Daniel has nearly reached its complete fulfillment. Soon the scenes of trouble spoken of in the prophecies will take place.[34]

In the light of Ellen White's statements concerning last-day events (see *The Shape of the Coming Crisis*), it appears that when she speaks of the "world . . . [being] stirred by the spirit of war" and "the scenes of trouble," she is not speaking of armed conflict between nation and nation but the persecution of God's people by the nations. Notice how the next statement confirms this conclusion:

Troublous times are before us. The world is stirred with the spirit of war. Soon the scenes of trouble spoken of in the prophecies will take place. The prophecy in the eleventh [chapter] of Daniel has nearly reached its complete fulfillment. Much of the history that has taken place in the fulfillment of this prophecy will be repeated. In the thirtieth verse a power is spoken of that "shall be grieved, and return, and have indignation against the holy covenant: so shall he do; he shall even return, and have intelligence with them that forsake the holy covenant. [Verses 31-36 quoted.][35]

Observe that troublous times are "before *us*." Thus, the "war" Ellen White speaks of is not necessarily armed conflict between nations. As shown above, it is far more likely she is speaking of the persecution of God's people by the nations and, as previously pointed out, she is simply using military terminology. Notice also that "much of the history" of the prophecy of Daniel 11:30-36 "will be repeated." She continues:

> Scenes similar to those described in these words will take place. We see evidence that Satan is fast obtaining the control of human minds who have not the fear of God before them.[36]

Here are some of the things that have happened in the past which apparently will be repeated in the future:

Daniel 11:31 speaks of the polluting of the sanctuary. This the papacy has done in ages past by "taking away" Christ's mediation in the heavenly sanctuary and substituting in its place the sacrifice of the mass. If this portion of the prophecy is to be repeated, it probably refers to attacks in the last days on our doctrine of the sanctuary.[37]

Speaking marvelous things against the God of gods refers to the papacy's claim that the Roman pontiff is God on earth.[38] It would be nothing new if these claims, not expressed openly at present, are repeated in the future. Ellen White continues:

> Let all read and understand the prophecies of this book, for we are now entering upon the time of trouble spoken of: "And at that time shall Michael stand up, the great prince which standeth for the children of thy people: and there shall be a time of trouble, such as never was since there was a nation even to that same time: and at that time thy people shall be delivered, every one that shall be found written in the book. [The quotation continues to verse 4.]...
>
> The Spirit of the Lord is being withdrawn from the world. It is no time now for men to exalt themselves.[39]

The book Ellen White is referring to is, of course, the book of Daniel, which will doubtless be better understood when the prophecies of the 11th chapter, verses 30-36, have their "final fulfillment."

The final withdrawal of God's Spirit takes place when Michael stands up, in other words, when probation closes.[40]

The fact that Ellen White states that the "power spoken of" "in the thirtieth verse" shall "have indignation against the holy covenant" clearly suggests that the persecutions the papacy carried out in the past will be repeated in the future when it unites with apostate Protestantism.[41] If so, these future events in some way, not clearly understood at present, harmonize with the events described in *GC,* pages 605-640; for the expression, "At that time shall Michael stand up" (Dan. 12:1) may also be rendered, "in that time" or "during that time." With this interpretation in mind, notice that according to Daniel 7:11, 2 Thess. 2:8, and Rev. 19:19, 20, the papal power endures until the Second Coming.

The Sequence of Events in *The Great Controversy*

The sequence of events described in *GC,* pages 605-640, begins with agitation in "the United States" for the enforcement of "Sunday observance" (something still in the future at this writing, 1998), followed by "the church" appealing "to the strong arm of civil power, . . . and papists and Protestants" uniting, thus reviving the papal power. This is followed by increasingly severe persecution (*GC,* pp. 607-631). (See *The Shape of the Coming Crisis.*)

The papacy has persecuted in the past.[42] Daniel 11:35 says that "some of them of understanding shall fall, to try them, and purge, and to make them white." This apparently refers to the time when the papal persecutions of the past are repeated.[43]

The standing up of Michael (Dan. 12:1) is described in *GC,* page 613. Adventists have interpreted this act as representing the cessation of Christ's "intercession in the sanctuary above," in other words, the close of human probation. In between agitation for Sunday legislation in the United States and the Second Coming, the battle over the law of God increases in intensity. It is probably during this interval that the scenario of Daniel 11:40–12:4 is played out. Exactly how this happens we probably will not know "until the unrolling of the scroll."[44] Without the sure word of prophecy to guide us, it behooves us not to engage in unwarranted speculation.

Will We Learn From the Past?

It was George Santayana who said: "Those who cannot remember the past are condemned to repeat it."[45] It is up to us to determine whether or not we shall profit from our past mistakes or are condemned to repeat them. The history of our interpretations of Armageddon and the king of the north are prime examples of the embarrassments we have brought on ourselves by following popular Protestant interpretations of prophecy and trying to be prophets rather than what God intended us to be—the proclaimers of *"the sure word of prophecy"* (2 Peter 1:19). Let us never forget *there is a difference.* Without the sure word of prophecy to guide us, we would do well to heed James White's caution to "tread lightly" when it comes to unfulfilled prophecy.

Hopefully, by reviewing some of our mistakes in the past we shall learn how to avoid them in the future. If this is what happens, this book will have achieved its purpose.

---

1. Arthur L. White, *The Lonely Years* (Hagerstown, Md.: Review and Herald Publishing Association,) p. 261. Quoting E. G. White Letter (abbrev. Lt) 59, 1884.
2. Lt 229, 1903, quoted in *Evangelism,* p. 366.
3. Ms 76, 1901, quoted in *21MR,* p. 444.
4. Uriah Smith, *Daniel and the Revelation: The Response of History to the Voice of Prophecy;*

A Verse by Verse Study of These Important Books of the Bible (Oakland, Calif.: Pacific Press Publishing Association, 1897), p. 400.

5. *RH,* April 5, 1906.

6. In 1901 Ellen White wrote concerning *D&R*: "This book has been the means of bringing many precious souls to a knowledge of the truth. Everything should be done to circulate *Thoughts on Daniel and the Revelation.* I know of no other book that can take the place of this one" (Ms 76, 1901, quoted in *Publishing Ministry,* p. 356). Apparently Ellen White endorsed Uriah Smith's *D&R* not because he always consistently applied this principle of interpretation, but because in general he presented Bible prophecy from the perspective of the great controversy.

7. Ms 13, 1889, quoted in *CWE,* pp. 30, 31.

8. See *1MR,* pp. [52]-59, "The 'Blocks' and 'Pins' of the Message," and pp. [160]-65, "Statements Regarding *Thoughts on Daniel and the Revelation.*"

9. Lt 16, 1900, quoted in *18MR,* pp. 22-24.

10. *RH,* Mar. 29, 1892, speaks of the time "when the outpouring of the Holy Spirit [the latter rain] will take place,—when the mighty angel [of Revelation 18] will come down from heaven, and unite with the third angel in closing up the work for this world." See the chapter, "The Loud Cry, the Angel of Revelation 18, and the Latter Rain," in *The Shape of the Coming Crisis,* available at your Adventist Book Center.

11. Lt 112, 1890, quoted in *14MR,* pp. 286-288.

12. Ms 7a, 1896, quoted in *14MR,* pp. 90-98.

13. *RH,* May 13, 1902.

14. Ms 172, 1899, quoted in *Seventh-day Adventist Bible Commentary* (Hagerstown, Md.: Review and Herald Publishing Association, 1957),vol. 7, p. 982. (abbrev. *7BC,* p. 982).

15. Ms 1a, 1890, quoted in *7BC,* p. 983.

16. *RH,* Jan. 27, 1885.

17. *ST,* Jan. 17, 1884. See "The Mark of the Beast and the Sunday Versus Sabbath Conflict" in *The Shape of the Coming Crisis.*

18. Ms 175, 1899, quoted in *19MR,* pp. 159, 160.

19. *GC,* pp. 611, 612, cf. p. 613.

20. For a further discussion concerning the events connected with the sixth and seventh plagues, see the chapter "The Close of Probation, the Plagues, and the Death Decree" in *The Shape of the Coming Crisis.*

21. *RH,* Oct. 19, 1897.

22. Lt 79, 1897, quoted in *7BC,* p. 967.

23. *RH,* Oct. 21, 1902, emphasis supplied.

24. *ST,* April 21, 1890.

25. *RH,* Mar. 18, 1884; *RH,* July 16, 1901. See the chapter "The Trials and Triumph of the Third Angel's Message" in *The Shape of the Coming Crisis.*

26. *ST,* Dec. 29, 1890.

27. *Education,* p. 176.

28. *RH,* Sept. 5, 1899. For a further discussion of this point, see the chapter "Deliverance, the Special Resurrection, and the Second Coming" in *The Shape of the Coming Crisis.*

29. Ellen White in *The Day Star* (abbrev. *DS*), Mar. 14, 1846, says: "I saw a flaming cloud

come where Jesus stood and he . . . took his place on the cloud, which carried him to the east, where it first appeared to the saints on earth." In *EW,* p. 15, she says: "Soon our eyes were drawn to the east, for a small black cloud had appeared, . . . which we all knew was the sign of the Son of Man."

30. *GC,* pp. 628, 629.
31. Ibid., pp. 635-637 emphasis supplied.
32. Ibid., pp. 654-656.
33. *RH,* Nov. 24, 1904.
34. *9T,* p. 14.
35. Lt 103, 1904, quoted in *13MR,* p. 394.
36. *Lt* 103, 1904.
37. The doctrine of the sanctuary is unique to Seventh-day Adventists. "In the future, deception of every kind is to arise. . . . The enemy will bring in false theories, such as the doctrine that there is no sanctuary" (*RH,* May 25, 1905).
38. E.g., "We hold upon this earth the place of God Almighty." Pope Leo XIII. Encyclical Letter, "The Reunion of Christendom," dated June 20, 1894, translated in *The Great Encyclical Letters of Leo XIII* (New York: Benziger [Roman Catholic], 1903), p. 304. Quoted in *Bible Students' Source Book,* Don F. Neufeld and Julia Neuffer, eds. (Hagerstown Md.: Review and Herald Publishing Association, 1962), p. 684, extract no. 1132.
39. Lt 103, 1904, quoted in *13MR,* p. 394.
40. *GC,* p. 613. Cf. *EW,* p. 36.
41. In *GC,* p. 578 Ellen White says: "[The] records of the past clearly reveal the enmity of Rome toward the true Sabbath and its defenders, and the means she employs to honor the institution of her creating. The word of God teaches that these scenes are to be repeated as Roman Catholics and Protestants shall unite for the exaltation of Sunday." In Ms 6, 1889 (quoted in *Selected Messages,* bk. 3, p. 387), she says: "The persecutions of Protestants by Romanism . . . will be more than rivaled, when Protestantism and popery are combined." For a fuller discussion of this persecution see "The Trials and Triumph of the Third Angel's Message" in *The Shape of the Coming Crisis.*
42. "No religion in the world (not a single one in the history of mankind) [sic] has on its conscience so many millions of people who thought differently, believed differently. Christianity is the most murderous religion there has ever been." This is stated by Catholic theologians Thomas and Gertrude Sartory in *"In der Hölle Brennt Kein Feur"* (Munich, 1968), pp. 88, 89, as quoted by H. Kung, *Eternal Life?* (Garden City, NY, 1984), p. 132. See *Symposium on Revelation,* Frank B. Holbrook, ed. (Silver Spring, Md.: Biblical Research Institute, 1992), vol. 7, bk. 2, p. 169.
43. *5T,* pp. 449, 450, which says: "Throughout the land the papacy is piling up her lofty and massive structures, in the secret recesses of which her former persecutions will be repeated."
44. *6T,* p. 17
45. *The Life of Reason,* vol. 2, quoted in John Bartlett, *Familiar Quotations* (Boston: Little, Brown and Company, 1980), 15th ed., p. 703.

Know What's Coming

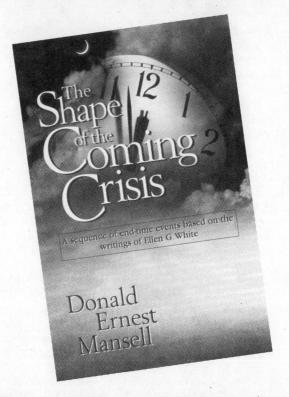

If you're overwhelmed by the massive jumble of end-time events information, *The Shape of the Coming Crisis*, by Donald Ernest Mansell, will help you make sense of it all. Based on the writings of Ellen White, this book reveals the chronological sequence of events heralding the long-awaited return of Christ. *The Shape of the Coming Crisis* will not only help you know what to expect in the future, it will help you to be prepared.

0-8163-1402-0, paperback.
US$12.99, Cdn$18.99